ONE TEAM. ONE GOAL.
MISSION ACCOMPLISHED.

BY JOHN HAREAS
PHOTOGRAPHY BY NBA ENTERTAINMENT PHOTOS

Published by EventDay Media & NBA Entertainment

CONTENTS

ONE TEAM. ONE GOAL.
MISSION ACCOMPLISHED.

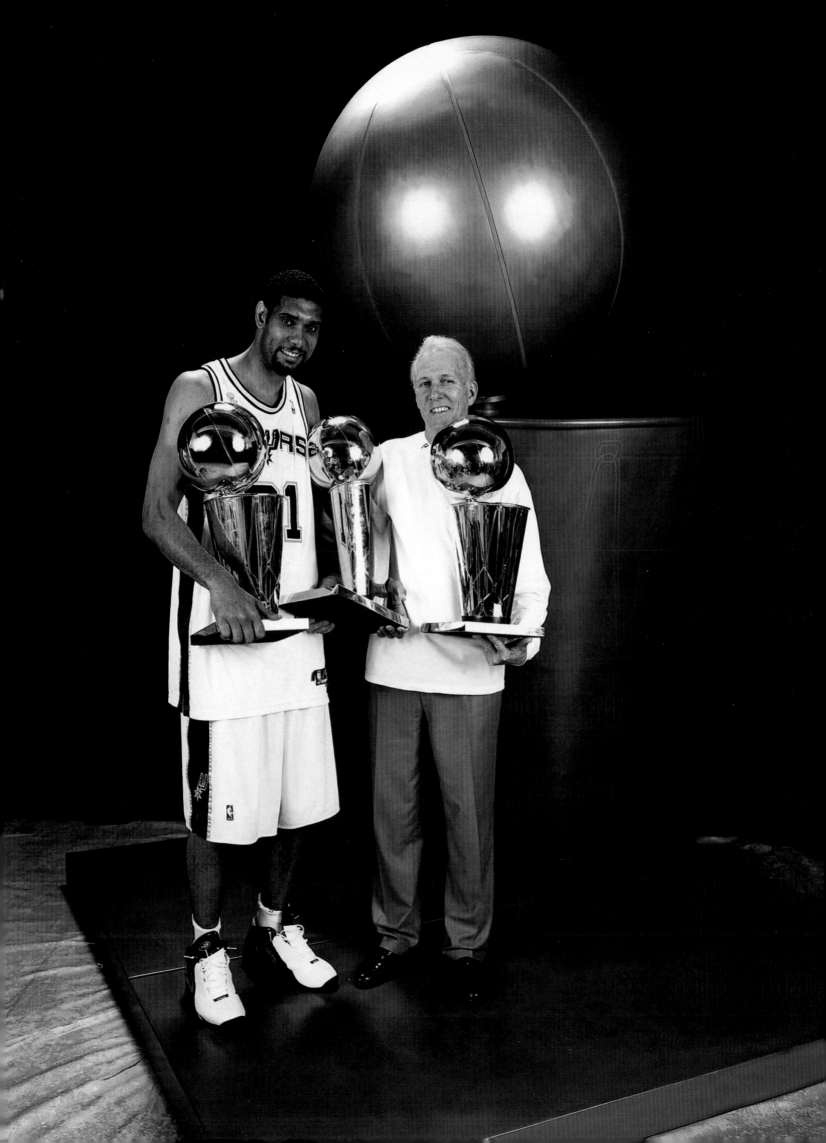

To Steve and Anastasia (mom and dad): Thank you for the love, support and education — J.H.

ACKNOWLEDGEMENTS

One team. One goal. Mission accomplished. It's not only the Spurs' championship philosophy, it's one that was fully embraced by NBA Entertainment and Event Day Media … *I'll be the roundabout. The words will make you out 'n' out …* Leading the championship parade down Harmon Meadow Boulevard was Charlie Rosenzweig, who grabbed a page out of Gregg Popovich's book and demanded that everyone on the NBAE side of this project "get over themselves" in producing the best possible commemorative … *And the wizards play down on Pinball Way on the boardwalk way past dark …* Similar to Finals MVP Tim Duncan, Joe Amati willed this terrific photography team highlighted by supreme go-to guys Brian Choi, John Kristofick, Bennett Renda and David Bonilla through a hard-fought seven-game series, scouring more than 4,000 images per game, in which the very best came to life on these pages … *Yeah a local hero he used to live here for a while …* The Ann Arbor legend via Livingston, N.J., Michael Levine, who, similarly to R.C. Buford, deftly handled all details of this massive project, particularly the marketing … *Driving in to Darlington County …* At EventDay Media, Tom Pokorny couldn't have been nicer and more patient as we all rode the wildly dramatic shifts of this classic series, while Tammy Davis flawlessly pulled it all together on the production end. Michelle Fusillo and the other extremely talented designers at EventDay Media, George Burgess, Adam Gilardi and Arla Fiorenzi impressed time and time again with high-energy layouts … *For the words I was sayin' …* Ron Koch at EventDay Media served as the ultimate point man, reviewing all editorial and handling all questions and delivering answers on a 24/7 basis… *They're doin' the E Street Shuffle …* To Alex Tarshis, Alex Woodson and Rob Crane for assisting yours truly on the fact-checking side … *And the highway she's deserted down to Breaker's Point …* Once again, Andy Bernstein, Nat Butler and Jesse Garrabrant, who delivered peak performance on command throughout the season and playoffs … *I am the Iceman …* George Gervin for his kindness and terrific insight … *Here's to the hearts and the hands of the men and women …* Gregg Popovich, R.C. Buford, Lawrence Payne, Bruce Guthrie, Tom James and Moe Guerrero for providing us with terrific access and assistance and couldn't have been any classier … *'Cause my love grows stronger …* To Jennifer, Emma, Christopher and our latest Lottery Pick, Leah, Thank you, Thank you, Thank you!!!!! … — John Hareas, July 2005

PHOTOGRAPHY CREDITS

Andrew D. Bernstein: Front Cover, Back Cover, 5, 6, 20, 31, 38, 44, 46, 48-49, 52, 54, 55, 56, 60, 61, 65, 66, 67, 68, 69, 71, 72, 73, 74, 76, 78, 82, 83, 86, 91, 92, 93, 94, 96, 97, 101, 104, 106, 107, 109, 110, 111 **Nathaniel S. Butler:** Front Cover, Back Cover, 3, 41, 44, 45, 50, 51, 53, 55, 57, 59, 63, 64, 65, 66, 70, 71, 72, 73, 77, 79, 80, 83, 84-85, 86, 87, 89, 92, 97, 100, 102, 103, 104-105, 106, 108, 111, 112 **Jesse D. Garrabrant:** Front Cover, 1, 7, 26, 39, 48, 54, 55, 62, 66, 67, 81, 92, 93, 95, 105, 106, 110 **Terrence Vaccaro:** 61, 64 **Chris Birck:** 14, 18, 21, 25, 28, 32, 34, 37, 39, 41, 42, 43, 52, 59, 66, 67 **Noah Graham:** 16, 35, 52, 58, 88-89, 99 **Joe Murphy:** 17, 22, 39 **D. Clarke Evans:** Back Cover, 8, 10, 12, 13, 17, 18, 19, 21, 22, 28-29, 32, 33, 36, 37, 39, 41, 44, 66, 67 **David Sherman:** 22 **Rocky Widner:** 24, 26 **Gregory Shamus:** 28, 75, 81, 86, 87, 90 **Glenn James:** 23, 28, 32 **Chris Covatta:** 18, 30, 66, 98 **Jeff Reinking:** 25, 30, 44 **Garrett W. Ellwood:** 15, 30, 35, 40-41, 42 **Brian Babineau:** 32 **Bill Baptist:** 32, 36, 37 **Barry Gossage:** 36, 46, 47 **Allen Einstein:** 39, 79, 92, 93 **Victor Baldizon:** 27 **Layne Murdoch:** Front Cover, 8, 11, 98, 107 **David Liam Kyle:** 15, 18 **Dan Lippitt:** 79 Kent Smith: Gervin Sidebar pages 56, 64, 74, 82, 90, 100, 108 **NBA Photos:** 66 **Getty Images Brian Bahr:** Front Cover **Elsa:** 12 **Ronald Martinez:** 26, 111 **Taylor Jones:** 9, 10, 11, 12 **Stephen Dunn:** 66

PUBLISHED BY:
EventDay Media. 1801 W. International Speedway Blvd., Daytona Beach, FL 32114

SPECIAL THANKS

At NBAE Photos: Joe Amati, Brian Choi, David Bonilla, John Kristofick, Pam Costello, Bennett Renda, Victor Nicholson. AT NBAE: Adam Silver, Gregg Winik, Charlie Rosenzweig, Paul Hirschheimer, David Denenberg, Marc Hirschheimer, Michael Levine, Tony Stewart, Rob Sario, Mario Argote, Alex Woodson. AT THE NBA: David J. Stern, Russ Granik, Tim Andree, Brian McIntyre, Terry Lyons, Tim Frank. AT THE SPURS: Peter Holt, Gregg Popovich, R.C. Buford, Russ Bookbinder, Lawrence Payne, Danny Ferry, Bruce Guthrie, Tom James, Brian Facchini, Cliff Puchalski, Moe Guerrero and the entire Spurs Organization. AT EVENTDAY MEDIA: Tom Pokorny, Tammy Davis, Ron Koch, Michelle Fusillo, George Burgess, Cynthia Dusenbery, J.J. O'Malley, Arla Fiorenzi, Adam Gilardi, Lindsay Crozier, Pat Dreyer, Rob Wolf, John Schreiner, Vince Warren and Michelle Rowe.

2004-05 NBA CHAMPIONS DVD

Relive the excitement of The Finals with the Official 2004-05 NBA Champions DVD, featuring exclusive behind-the-scenes footage and interviews. From the season-opener to the Game 7 clincher, this special edition DVD highlights one of the greatest seasons in San Antonio Spurs history. Available wherever videos are sold.

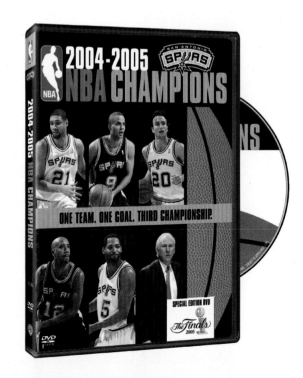

REFLECTIONS ON A
CHAMPIONSHIP JOURNEY

BY GREGG POPOVICH

"Wow. Gracias."

These were the words Manu Ginobili used to start his speech after being introduced during the Spurs championship celebration at the Alamodome.

I think he picked the two perfect words to capture the moment.

There are a few of us who have been fortunate enough to experience all three NBA championships. One thing is for sure, the parade on the San Antonio River and the celebration in the Dome will never get old.

After two hours on the river, we made our way to the Alamodome. Tired, you step off a trolley and walk onto the floor of the Dome. All of a sudden you feel a jolt of adrenaline surging through your body as you are greeted by 63,823 fans, each screaming at a level higher than they've ever screamed before.

As we approach the stage in the center of the Dome, it hits you. We are NBA champions. The journey is long, and most cannot endure the physical, mental, and emotional pitfalls. I congratulate this group of players for its persistent effort, resilient attitude and grace under fire (from opponents, media and me). You have truly accomplished what most will never realize, and I urge you to reflect on what was required.

The 2004-05 season lasted 105 games spanning 263 days. During the season, everyone associated with the team had tunnel vision. Each loss haunts us for weeks while a victory brings only moments of joy. Each of us gets so wrapped up in the season that we lose track of the wonderful moments along the way.

This playoff run was exceptionally satisfying, since each round offered opponents of extraordinary difficulty.

The Denver Nuggets were the hottest team in the league entering the playoffs, posting an NBA-best 25-4 record after the All-Star break. They proved to be extremely physical, and for us to win two games on the road made it a very satisfying and confidence-building series.

The Seattle SuperSonics were an unusually difficult team to play, since they displayed a physical inside game with a let-it-fly attitude in transition. As the series progressed, we figured out a way to win, but it was never easy.

The Phoenix Suns presented the classic matchup of offense versus defense, and with impressive credentials: the league's most potent offense, the MVP, the Coach of the Year and the best record. Our Denver experience helped significantly as we started on the road and posted three wins in Phoenix, allowing us to win the series. Our offense really came together during the series and our confidence was at its highest point as we entered The Finals.

The Finals was one for the ages, and the games speak for themselves. Both teams were mentally and physically prepared and Games 5, 6 and 7 did not disappoint.

To have it all come down to a Game 7 in the NBA Finals is amazing and unforgettable.

Walking onto the court that night — June 23 — is a moment I'll never forget. You — our fans — are the best. We've always said that, and it's true, but that night the energy was at a level I've never experienced. When we were down nine points in the third quarter, there is no doubt that the boost we received from each of you gave the team that little extra we needed to get back into the game and finish off the reigning NBA champions.

Everyone played a part in this series to bring the championship back to San Antonio. So, to everyone involved — players, coaches, families, staff, ownership and fans — I think two simple words really sum it up.

Wow. Gracias.

Gregg Popovich

CHAMPIONS

Chants of "Go Spurs Go" punctuated the air as fans took their favorite spots along the world famous San Antonio Riverwalk. Diehards flocked four hours before the Spurs' Championship Celebration commenced to the Rivercenter Mall Laguna, securing a prime location to watch all 26 barges lazily float along the two-mile parade route.

A sea of Ginobili, Parker and Duncan jerseys were visible from balconies, cobblestone walkways and arched footbridges. Little did architect Robert Hugman know back in 1929 that his vision for the Riverwalk would also serve as the ultimate destination for a championship fiesta.

Celebrating greatness has become an annual tradition in the Alamo City. It is the third time in seven years — and second in three — that the faithful toasted this dynasty-in-the-making. More than 350,000 fans paid tribute to the 2005 NBA champions, who were more than happy to return the favor.

"I want you all to know that, especially in Game 7 when we went down nine, we needed everybody — in the bars, in the living room, in the arena — or it couldn't happen," Spurs head coach Gregg Popovich said. "That was great. All of your support is really important to us. It fuels us. A lot of times during the season you don't even know about, when we're losing a couple in a row and all that sort of stuff. We love the fact that you care about what we do, and we're always going to love you for it. Thank you for your support. We appreciate it."

Tim Duncan, who, 48 hours earlier, won his third NBA Finals Award and further cemented his legacy as one of the game's all-time greats, was accompanied by teammate Bruce Brown in barge No. 25 and gave the Spurs' faithful another huge assist.

"Thank you so much. Your support was so incredible. You gave us this incredible home-court advantage that we absolutely needed. You took us all the way to the top."

Robert Horry knows a thing or two about championship parades being a veteran of five of them when he played for the Houston Rockets and Los Angeles Lakers. "Big Shot Rob" found a permanent place in San Antonio lore with his amazing Game 5 performance in The Finals, forever endearing himself to the Spurs' faithful.

"I'm glad we can bring another championship to San Antonio," Horry said. "Most importantly, I'm so, so happy that you have accepted me as one of your own. When I first got here, I'd go

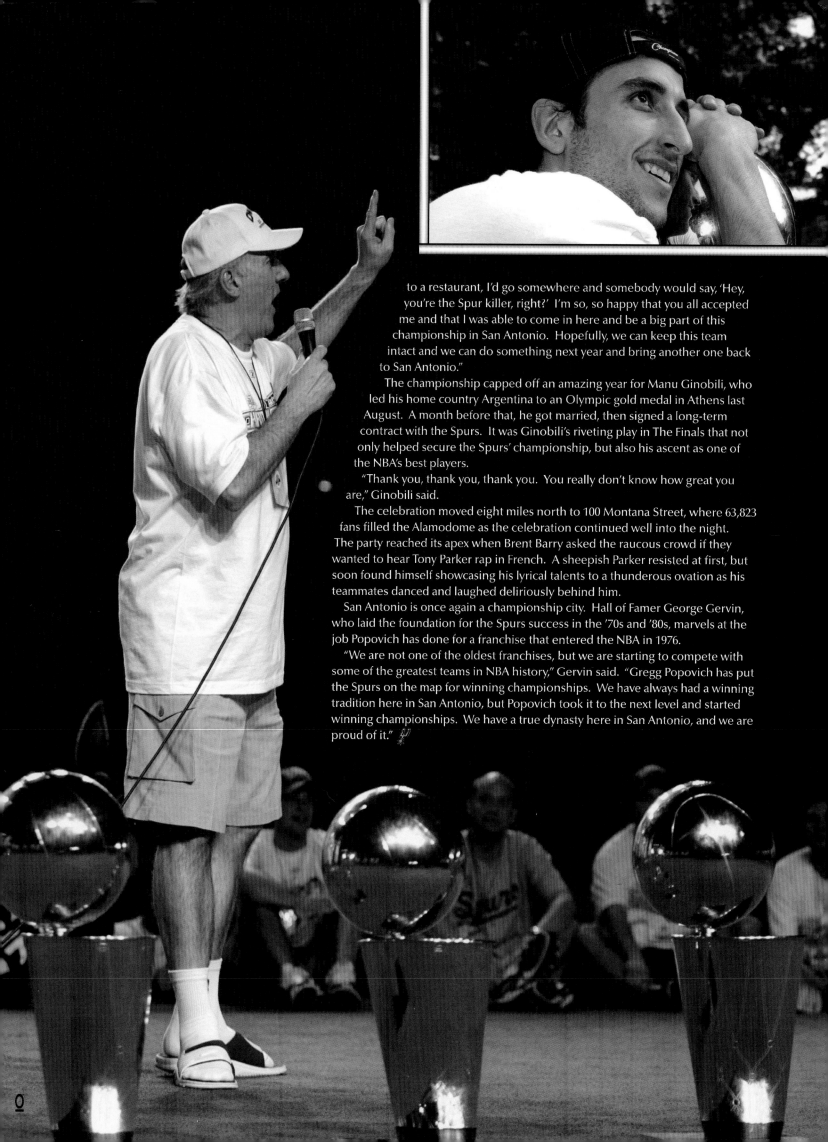

to a restaurant, I'd go somewhere and somebody would say, 'Hey, you're the Spur killer, right?' I'm so, so happy that you all accepted me and that I was able to come in here and be a big part of this championship in San Antonio. Hopefully, we can keep this team intact and we can do something next year and bring another one back to San Antonio."

The championship capped off an amazing year for Manu Ginobili, who led his home country Argentina to an Olympic gold medal in Athens last August. A month before that, he got married, then signed a long-term contract with the Spurs. It was Ginobili's riveting play in The Finals that not only helped secure the Spurs' championship, but also his ascent as one of the NBA's best players.

"Thank you, thank you, thank you. You really don't know how great you are," Ginobili said.

The celebration moved eight miles north to 100 Montana Street, where 63,823 fans filled the Alamodome as the celebration continued well into the night. The party reached its apex when Brent Barry asked the raucous crowd if they wanted to hear Tony Parker rap in French. A sheepish Parker resisted at first, but soon found himself showcasing his lyrical talents to a thunderous ovation as his teammates danced and laughed deliriously behind him.

San Antonio is once again a championship city. Hall of Famer George Gervin, who laid the foundation for the Spurs success in the '70s and '80s, marvels at the job Popovich has done for a franchise that entered the NBA in 1976.

"We are not one of the oldest franchises, but we are starting to compete with some of the greatest teams in NBA history," Gervin said. "Gregg Popovich has put the Spurs on the map for winning championships. We have always had a winning tradition here in San Antonio, but Popovich took it to the next level and started winning championships. We have a true dynasty here in San Antonio, and we are proud of it."

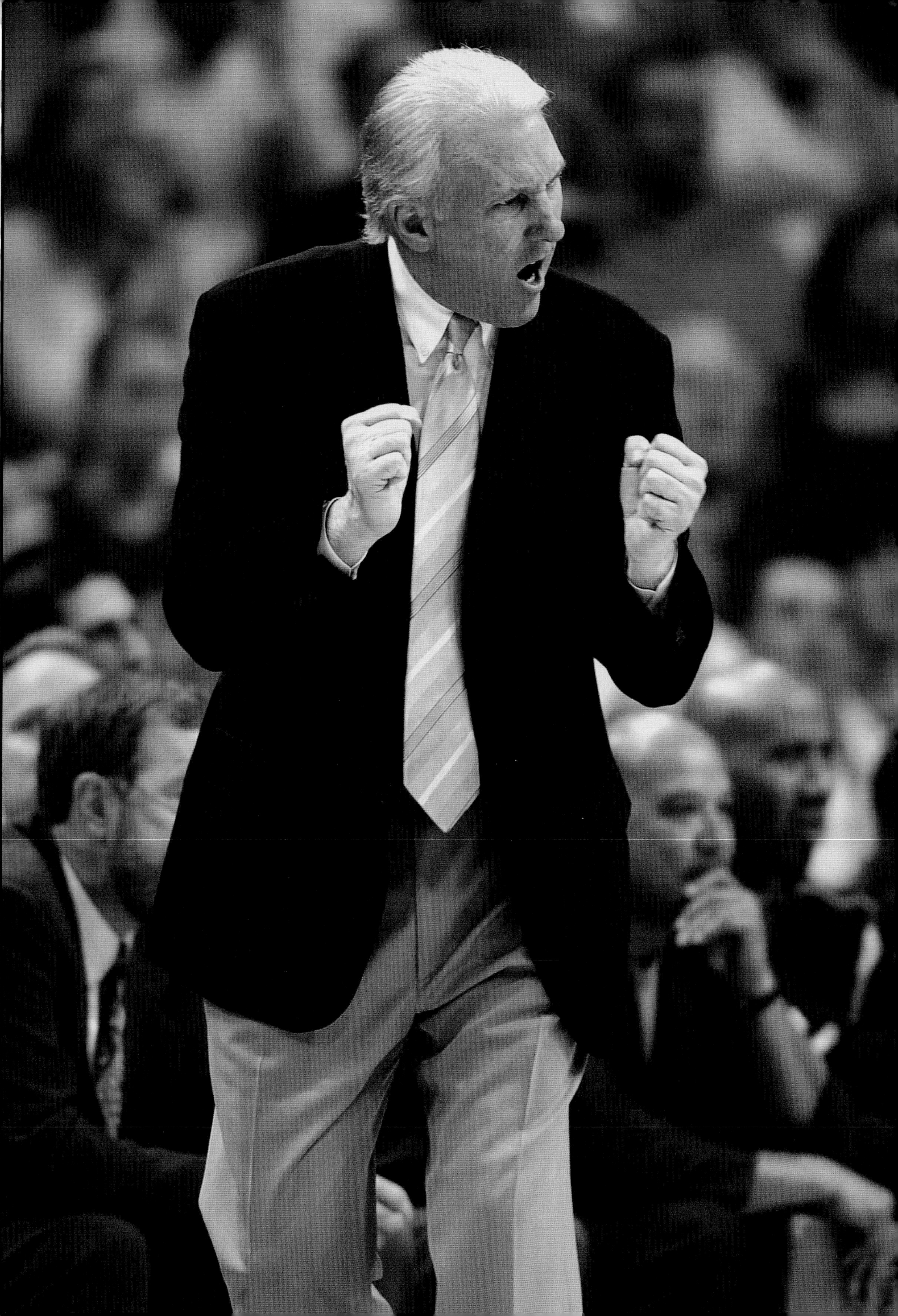

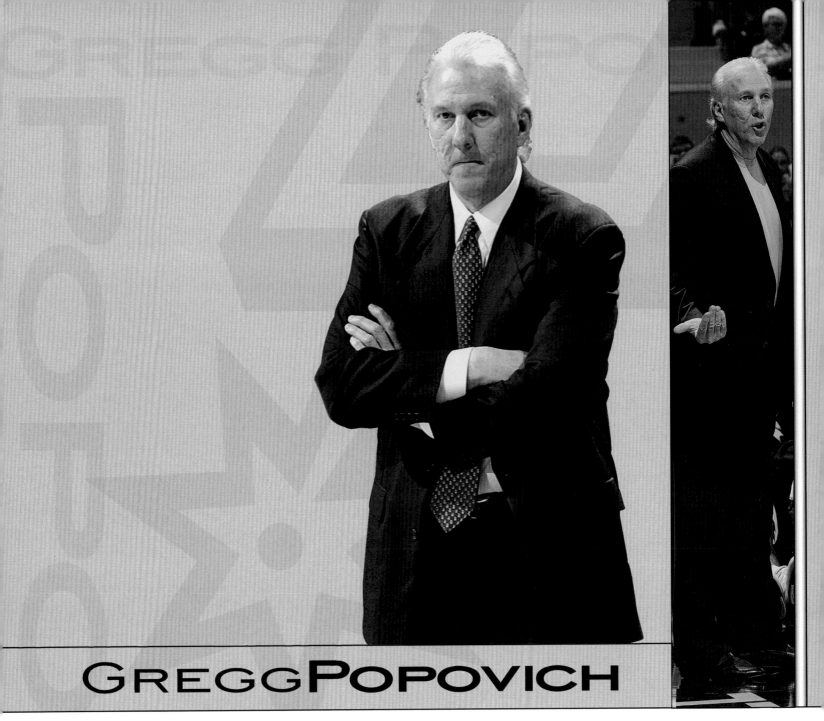

GREGG POPOVICH

Gregg Popovich will never say it, publicly or privately. It's doubtful that he seriously even ponders the subject. Instead, his NBA résumé will have to do the talking. Otherwise, maybe one of his many admirers in the coaching fraternity — or a basketball legend who has stood at the feet of coaching genius and recognizes greatness when he sees it — will have to give praise.

Discussions about success must begin with anyone but Popovich, a man who not only adheres to, but embodies a "get over yourself" motto he learned at the Air Force Academy. A motto he demands his players embrace.

Asking Popovich about his membership in the NBA coaching elite is likely to draw a terse, "next question" or "nobody cares, let's talk about Iraq or something that matters" response.

What does matter in determining coaching greatness in the NBA, and, ultimately, a place in

the Naismith Memorial Basketball Hall of Fame, is building and leading a team to three championships with different rosters minus Tim Duncan. And, that only four other men in NBA history — Red Auerbach (nine), Phil Jackson (nine), John Kundla (five) and Pat Riley (four) — have won more titles than you.

Sorry, Gregg Popovich, you're in rarified company.

"Gregg Popovich is the best coach in the NBA," Hall of Famer Bill Walton said. "I was privileged to play for six coaches who are in the Naismith Memorial Basketball Hall of Fame, and Gregg Popovich is the coach in today's game that I would most want to play for. He is responsible for everything that goes down in the league's most successful, respected and admired franchise."

Off the court, the brilliant personnel moves can be traced to Popovich's military background when he majored in Soviet Studies at the Air Force Academy. Not only did Popovich play all four years, he also traveled to Eastern Europe and the Soviet Union as a member of the U.S. Armed Forces Team, gaining a global perspective on the talent that existed outside the United States' borders.

"The opportunities I got in the military to travel with basketball really made me understand how much basketball is played around the world, how many good players there are," Popovich said.

The tour of duty served Popovich and the Spurs well when he was named the team's general manager in 1994. Nearly 25 years after his travels, it isn't a

coincidence that the Spurs feature the NBA's most international team. With five players hailing from outside the United States, the Spurs outsmarted their fellow NBA teams with such draft-day steals as Manu Ginobili (57th), Tony Parker (28th) and Beno Udrih (28th).

On the court, the 2003 NBA Coach of the Year is lauded for his X's and O's strategy, defensive philosophy and attention to detail in preparing his team. It's also no coincidence that during this season's march toward the championship, Popovich became the fifth-fastest coach in NBA history to win 400 games — the only ones to do it faster are Riley, Jackson, K.C. Jones and Billy Cunningham. Yet, it is his consistent, tough-love approach of getting his players — all 12 of them — to reach their potential that may be his coaching trademark.

"He's not afraid to tell anything to anybody," Ginobili said. "He doesn't care if it's Tim Duncan or the player that is on the injured reserve. Everybody appreciates that, because there are many coaches who never tell the star what to do. Everybody feels it's the same situation. It's really good for the spirit of the team."

Spurs reserve forward Robert Horry agrees.

The six-time NBA champion, who has played under Rudy Tomjanovich with the Houston Rockets and Jackson with the Los Angeles Lakers, said there is an underlying goal in Popovich's approach.

"Pop just wants the best out of you," Horry said. "He's going to be on you hard — I mean really hard — so, if you have the mental toughness to take that, you're going to develop as a player."

Popovich coached eight years at Pomona-Pitzer in Clarement, California, before accepting a volunteer assistant position with Larry Brown at Kansas in 1986. He then followed Brown down to San Antonio the next year as an assistant coach. Popovich is effusive in his praise of Brown for not only giving him his start but also ingraining the "play-the-right-way" philosophy.

"I wouldn't be standing here if it wasn't for Larry Brown," Popovich said during the Larry O'Brien Trophy ceremony at center court after Game 7 of the Finals. "He's the best."

Just don't ask Popovich about his place in history. You're better off asking someone else.

"Gregg Popovich represents the purest sense of coaching," Walton said. "He is a teacher, and not so much of basketball skills as in the game of life. We never hear a word of hype, self-promotion or egomania from Gregg Popovich. It is always about the truest ideals of the human spirit. Gregg Popovich is always the first to say how lucky he is to coach David Robinson, Tim Duncan, Sean Elliot, Avery Johnson and, now, Manu Ginobili and Robert Horry.

"He always says how fortunate he is to work with the Spurs and to be in the NBA. The fact of the matter is, the game, the NBA and the Spurs are better off because of Gregg Popovich," Walton said. "We are the lucky ones."

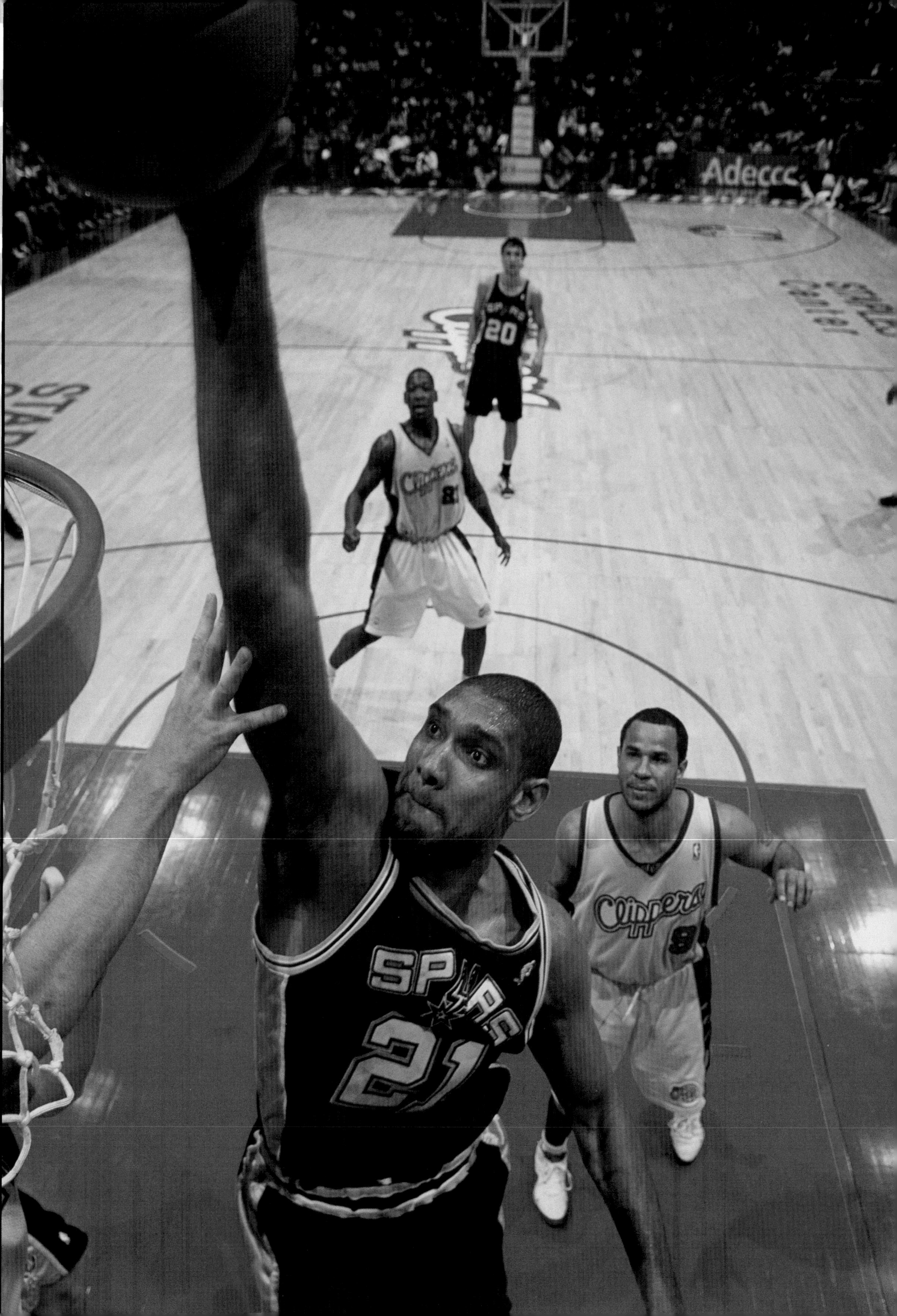
20
Clippers
Clippers
21

TIMDUNCAN

His basketball legacy is far from complete. Not at the age of 29, when he is in the prime of his career and has three NBA championships and three Finals MVPs on his résumé. When Tim Duncan retires, ultimately, he will be judged not by his unassuming nature, stoic demeanor or the fact that he doesn't provide reporters great sound bites, but rather he'll be evaluated by the number of championships his teams have won. Like all legends are.

"I think the great players' legacies all are built around that, how many championships they have, whether they were the MVP of the deal, how did they play in the important games," Spurs head coach Gregg Popovich said. "I think that's true."

The third NBA title places Duncan in a select group along with Magic Johnson, Michael Jordan and Shaquille O'Neal as the only players to win three or more Finals MVP Awards since it was

first issued in 1969. How many championships did those greats compile by age 29? Johnson had five, while Jordan and O'Neal had two each. Those players also called Kareem Abdul-Jabbar, James Worthy, Scottie Pippen and Kobe Bryant teammates during their championship runs.

While Duncan won his first two titles with a future first ballot Hall-of-Famer in David Robinson, the 2005 NBA title places the two-time NBA MVP in ultra-exclusive company. The only other player to win an NBA championship with an entire set of new teammates was 11-time NBA champion Bill Russell when he led the Boston Celtics to a seven-game series triumph over the Los Angeles Lakers in 1969. Other than Duncan, not one member of the Spurs' 1999 championship team hoisted the Larry O'Brien Trophy over their heads in 2005.

"There is no question that Tim Duncan is going to be a Hall-of-Famer," said Willis Reed, who won two NBA Finals MVP Awards in leading the New York Knicks to two championships in the 1970's. "He is going to go down as one of the great, all-time skilled big men. He probably does not get as much recognition or publicity because he plays in San Antonio, but there is no question that he learned well under the tutelage of David Robinson. He has taken his game to another level and he has proven that he has great leadership ability."

It is an attribute that didn't come easily for Duncan who was thrust into that role when Robinson retired after the 2003 title.

"I had to learn," Duncan said. "I wasn't asked to be a leader early on in my

career. I was allowed to learn through time, and just in watching the guys around me and in front of me. So, it's not something that came natural."

That leadership ability was tested like never before in Duncan's eight-year NBA career when he and his teammates faced their ultimate challenge entering Game 7 of the Finals against the defending champion Detroit Pistons. The legacy of two NBA titles, two NBA MVP Finals Awards was surprisingly being questioned after three consecutive sub-par games — by Duncan's standards — in which he averaged less than 20 points while missing crucial free throws down the stretch, totaling only 15-of-30 from the line.

Yet Duncan came through in the most crucial time — the third quarter with his team trailing by nine. He led his teammates with a 12-point and six-rebound performance that triggered an 18-7 run and sent the Spurs on their way to the title. Duncan's 25 points, 11 rebounds and two blocks points the very definition of a clutch performance in the biggest game of his career — and, he did it in his undemonstrative, workmanlike way that included making five of six free throws late in Game 7.

"Some people knocked him because he did not make his free throws," Reed said, "but, in Game 7, when he had to make them and when he had to be the dominant player, Tim did what he had to do to win."

It's been quite a storied career for the St. Croix native, who was the No. 1 pick in the 1997 NBA Draft. Since his arrival, the Spurs own the best record in the NBA, going 438-186, while boasting the best winning-percentage of any team in the four major sports. When he earned yet another All-NBA First Team selection following the 2004-05 season, Duncan became only the fifth player in the NBA to receive such an honor in his first eight seasons, joining Hall-of-Famers Larry Bird, George Mikan, Bob Pettit and Oscar Robertson.

"Tim has been a key for the Spurs for his whole time there," said Abdul-Jabbar, owner of six NBA championship rings. "When he gets into The Finals, he has been very successful and it has not mattered who he has been playing with. It is a testament to his consistency. He is certainly one of the best frontline players to come along in the game. To be able to dominate the game like he has for the length of time he has is proof of his talent and consistency."

Despite the enormous success, Duncan is the same down-to-earth player as he was when he first arrived in San Antonio.

"He's basically an introverted, quite humorous, highly intelligent, easy-going guy who has gotten over himself," Popovich said. "He's not that impressed with himself. He just likes playing ball, and he goes home and does whatever he does. That's him."

With three NBA championships in five years, some are looking at the long-term legacy these Spurs will leave. With Duncan at 29, Manu Ginobili at 27 and Tony Parker at 23 and the excellent talent evaluation skills of general manager R.C. Buford and Popovich, the Spurs look to be in championship contention for years to come.

Beware, NBA teams and basketball legends.

"In years past, we've lost six, seven, eight, nine guys in a year and rebuilt," Duncan said. "I think we've really got a core here that we're in love with — that obviously is a pretty decent core — and we're going to have it together for a couple of years."

ManuGinobili
CONTROLLED CHAOS

He may be the greatest draft-day steal in modern NBA history. Fifty-six players were selected ahead of Manu Ginobili on June 30, 1999. In less than three NBA seasons, the 27-year-old Argentinean has made a lot of NBA general managers regret their oversight.

Thing the Spurs predicted such greatness? Think again.

"The draft came along, and it was in the 50s [late in the second round]," San Antonio Spurs head coach Gregg Popovich said. "And, there was nobody who was going to make our team there anyway, and this guy was the most athletic, so we said, 'Let's draft him.' But, we did not know he was going to become what he is today — that would have been a real stretch."

What isn't a stretch is Ginobili's value to the Spurs, especially this season. After filling a valuable reserve role in his first two campaigns,

Ginobili thrived in 2004-05, serving as the team's secondary scoring threat alongside two-time NBA MVP Tim Duncan. Ginobili enjoyed his first All-Star season, posting career-high averages in points (16), field-goal percentage (.471) and three-point percentage (.376), all while playing with the same frenzied, fast-paced style that continues to befuddle opponents, coaches and — yes — his teammates.

"A very different game," teammate Brent Barry said in describing Ginobili's style. "He is so awkward and just takes bizarre steps. Nothing seemingly fundamental ... but it works. He is so effective."

Even Ginobili can't pinpoint the loosey-goosey style of play that has been instrumental in the Spurs recent success.

"Oh, I have no clue," Ginobili said. "I always played kind of like this, crazy and unpredictable. But, it turned more like this while I was 18, 19. Before then, I wasn't like this. When I was 19, I was worse than this. My coaches, they used to get so upset — sometimes happy, but sometimes so upset. I don't know, but it comes from somewhere. It is probably how I feel the game."

Even though Popovich allows Manu to be Manu, he has seen growth in Ginobili's game in terms of harnessing his talent and making better decisions.

"If 'control' means playing smarter and with more wisdom," Popovich said, "I guess he plays more controlled, but his pace hasn't slowed. When I think of control, I think

ANY SPA CE. ANY PLACE. BELZ.COM

of pace. He's got the same frenetic pace about him that he's always had. But, he does not get himself into the same predicaments he used to, and, if he does, he seems to extricate himself more frequently, if that makes any sense."

Familiarity with the NBA opposition also has paid dividends in Ginobili's overall improvement.

"Now, he knows who is underneath and who can block shots — and, when it is too darned crowded in the lane," Popovich said. "He knows that this guy is pretty quick, and this is when I can pull up and shoot, or I'm going to give it up."

Things weren't always this way, Popovich said.

"Before, he would be going at people — go past these two people, between these two people, come hell or high water — but, he realizes who's a good defender, who's a bad defender, what's the time on the clock, what's

the score. Those things enter into his judgment, and he plays with more wisdom."

Ginobili's road to NBA success was far from traditional. After being selected by the Spurs in 1999, the 6-foot-6-inch guard played three more seasons in the Italian League where he earned league MVP honors twice, and, in one season, led Virtus Bologna to the championship and Euroleague Finals, where he also picked up MVP honors. In 2002, Ginobili helped his native country, Argentina, take the silver medal in the World Championship.

It's been quite a 12-month ride for the international superstar. Not only did he play a key role in the Spurs 2005 championship run after signing a six-year contract extension, he also led Argentina in winning the gold medal at the 2004 Summer Olympics in Athens, Greece. He averaged 19.3 points per game while shooting better than 57 percent from the field. That success served as a springboard for his most memorable NBA season yet.

"I think it really made him feel like he belongs in the top echelon of players on this planet," Popovich said. "Not that he would ever act like that or say that to you, but, I think, deep down in his gut, he knows that he is one hell of a competitor, and he knows what it takes to win." ✒

I LOVE THIS GAME?

La NBA tiene 13 latinos en sus filas, pero sólo ha hecho buen negocio en México. Con más partidos, campamentos y nuevos productos, las cosas mejorarán. Pero no espere un juego millonario.

Arly Faundes Berkhoff
Santiago

EL ROSTRO DE EMMANUEL "Manu" Ginobili ilumina la Avenida Paseo Colón, frente a la Plaza San Martín, en el centro de Buenos Aires. La gigantografía publicitaria con la estrella del básquet, tiene un lugar tan importante en la capital argentina como entre sus fanáticos. Muchos niños y jóvenes ya desfilan por todo el país con la camiseta del escolta, la "20" de los San Antonio Spurs.

La NBA ingresó a fines de 2004 a Argentina, donde ya tiene 120 puntos de venta de productos licenciados. El arribo fue empujado por el rebote económico y el buen histo-rial basquetbolístico argentino. La selección fue subcampeona en Indianápolis 2002 y medalla dorada en los Juegos Olímpicos de Atenas 2004. Sus equipos y jugadores se llenan por Sudamérica y Europa. Y Manu, Carlos Delfino (Detroit Pistons) y Andrés Nocioni (Chicago Bulls), que sucedieron a la NBA a José Sánchez y Rubén Wolkovi-sky, esperan por otros dos compatriotas en el próximo draft. Si a eso sumas que Manu ya ganó su primer anillo con los Spurs en 2003, tendrá en Argentina un caldo de cultivo ganador y en Manu, a la mayor figura regional para que la NBA explote.

Porque ése es el cuento: incluso con Manu y otros 12 latinoamericanos peleando escena, la NBA aún no cuaja como negocio

8.000 puntos de venta latinoamericanos. No es mucho, pero tampoco definitivo, pues David Stern, el comisionado de la liga, tiene un plan regional para mover más productos en las calles, eventos, campamentos y, desde de 2007, partidos de equipos de la liga que deberían mejorar sus marcas.

TIRO FALLIDO. Mientras, ¿por qué la bola no entra? Un problema crítico para el creci-miento de la liga han sido las crisis econó-micas regionales. Entre 2001 y 2002, las ventas de productos NBA crecieron un 67% en América Latina, pero se despertaron a una tasa del 10% un año después y recién volvie-ron a crecer un 31% en 2004. Para este año, la oficina latinoamericana de la NBA, en Miami, pronostica que los ingresos subirán un 19%, hasta unos US$ 36 millones, según cifras extraoficiales.

La crisis ha hecho que la liga maneje con mano de seda la explotación regional de su marca y referentes, algo a todas luces insuficiente. De hecho, hasta ahora, quien mejores resultados ha dado a la NBA no fueron los campeones olímpicos argentinos ni Maybner "Nenê" Hilario, estrella de Bra-sil, la otra potencia basquetbolística regio-nal, sino el mexicano Eduardo Nájera. El Gigante de Chihuahua, compañero de Nenê en Denver Nuggets, es un alero producti-vo, pero miembro de una selección y un equipo sin gran ornato. Sin embargo, él ha ayudado a que México, dueño de un flujo

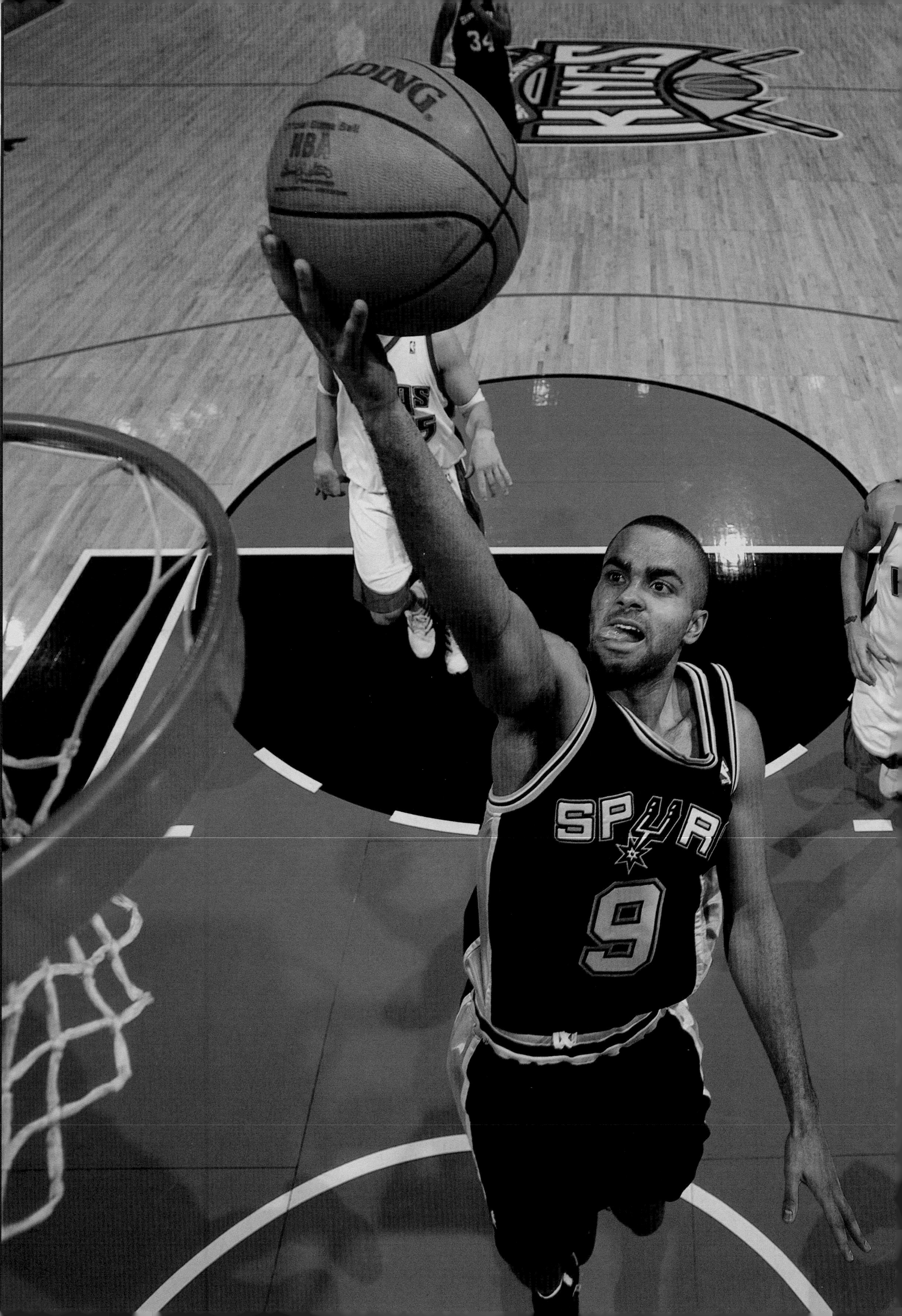

TONY PARKER
FRENCH REVOLUTION

He was Tony Parker's first NBA mentor. A man who saw a 19-year-old basketball prodigy arrive from the French basketball league full of potential and lightning-quick moves.

The year was 2001. The Belgium-born point guard drafted 28th overall by the San Antonio Spurs eagerly awaited the chance to make his mark. Terry Porter, a veteran of 17 NBA seasons and one of the most successful point guards of his era, settled into the twilight of his career.

The 38-year-old took the rookie under his wing and showed him the NBA ropes before retiring following the 2001-02 season. The former head coach of the Milwaukee Bucks, Porter is nearly four years removed from that first meeting in Spurs training camp.

"As the years have gone on, his confidence obviously has gotten higher, and I think that's the biggest thing," Porter said. "He's built the confidence from his teammates — the trust and respect from his teammates that he's going to do the right thing.

"His game itself has grown, also, because of his ability to make shots now. He struggled in that area. Most point guards struggle coming in — not many come in with a fine-tuned jump shot. You just don't see that, especially a guy like him who was basically coming out of high school, 18, 19 years old. So there was a lot of growth in that area that he needed, and he's obviously improved tremendously."

Thrust into duty his rookie season ahead of veterans Antonio Daniels and Porter, Parker made a seamless transition playing against NBA veteran competition — thanks to his extensive international league experience.

Parker spent four seasons in the French League, including two with Centre Federal, and averaged 22.1 points in only his second season at age 16. A year later, he found himself playing for Paris Racing, in the first division, and, in only his second season, he entered the starting lineup.

"Playing professionally helped me mature faster," Parker said. "I was playing with guys who were 30 years old and had families. I had to grow up fast and learn how to handle myself. I also had to learn to get respect."

Parker enjoyed a breakout campaign in only his second season, when he helped lead the Spurs to the 2003 NBA championship. Leading the team in assists, Parker finished second to Tim Duncan in scoring and opened a lot of eyes with his stellar play against All-NBA point guard Jason Kidd in the Finals.

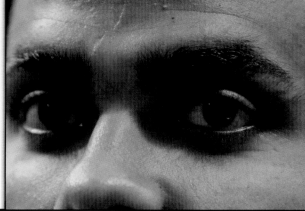

The maturation and development continued this year in Parker's fourth NBA season. He enjoyed career high averages in points (16.6), assists (6.1) and shooting percentage (.482 percent) while guiding the Spurs to the NBA's second-best record, tying the Miami Heat at 59-23.

An All-Star berth should be around the corner for Parker. After all, name another point guard who has led his team to more regular-season wins (176) than Parker in the last three seasons. Or, one who has guided his team to two NBA titles in three years with more potentially on the way.

All-Star recognition or not, the most important endorsement Parker can recieve is from his coach, Gregg Popovich, who has watched the 23-year-old blossom in the last two seasons.

"I'm 10,000 times more comfortable with the ball in [Parker's] hands late than I was a couple of years ago," Popovich said. "He understands situations much better and sees people much better on the court. No matter what play we call, he reads things and sees other things on the court that might not be there with the play we called, which he wouldn't have seen a couple of years ago."

Despite the vote of confidence from his head coach, Parker remains his toughest critic.

"I think I'm coming a long way since my rookie year," said Parker, who signed a long-term contract before the season. "I've established myself as a starting point guard, and now getting closer and closer to the All-Star Game and feeling close to the best point guard in the league.

"I believe in myself [and] I am one of the best point guards, and I can compete against the best on any given night. But, I still think I've got a lot of improvement to do in my game."

That's a scary thought to the rest of the NBA, but Parker believes it.

"My outside shot can be a lot better; my three-point shot can be more consistent and my free throws, obviously, I need to improve," Parker said. "And, leadership-wise, I still can improve, and the more I'm going to know our guys, and the more we're going to play big games, I'm going to establish myself as a real point guard, to be the 'Little General' out there."

DRAFT DAY STEAL

THE SPURS FOUND THEIR MAN, TONY PARKER, WITH THE LAST PICK OF THE FIRST ROUND OF THE 2001 NBA DRAFT.

	TEAM	PLAYER	HIGH SCHOOL/ COLLEGE
1.	WASHINGTON	KWAME BROWN	GLYNN ACADEMY HIGH SCHOOL (GEORGIA)
2.	L.A. CLIPPERS	TYSON CHANDLER	DOMINGUEZ HIGH SCHOOL (CALIFORNIA)
3.	ATLANTA	PAU GASOL	F.C. BARCELONA (SPAIN)
4.	CHICAGO	EDDY CURRY	THORNWOOD HIGH SCHOOL (ILLINOIS)
5.	GOLDEN STATE	JASON RICHARDSON	MICHIGAN STATE
6.	VANCOUVER	SHANE BATTIER	DUKE
7.	NEW JERSEY	EDDIE GRIFFIN	SETON HALL
8.	CLEVELAND	DESAGANA DIOP	OAK HILL HIGH SCHOOL (VIRGINIA)
9.	DETROIT	RODNEY WHITE	CHARLOTTE
10.	BOSTON	JOE JOHNSON	ARKANSAS
11.	BOSTON	KEDRICK BROWN	OKALOOSA-WALTON COMMUNITY COLLEGE (FLORIDA)
12.	SEATTLE	VLADIMIR RADMANOVIC	FMP ZELEZNIK (YUGOSLAVIA)
13.	HOUSTON	RICHARD JEFFERSON	ARIZONA
14.	GOLDEN STATE	TROY MURPHY	NOTRE DAME
15.	ORLANDO	STEVEN HUNTER	DEPAUL
16.	CHARLOTTE	KIRK HASTON	INDIANA
17.	TORONTO	MICHAEL BRADLEY	VILLANOVA
18.	HOUSTON	JASON COLLINS	STANFORD
19.	PORTLAND	ZACH RANDOLPH	MICHIGAN STATE
20.	CLEVELAND	BRENDAN HAYWOOD	NORTH CAROLINA
21.	BOSTON	JOSEPH FORTE	NORTH CAROLINA
22.	ORLANDO	JERYL SASSER	SOUTHERN METHODIST
23.	HOUSTON	BRANDON ARMSTRONG	PEPPERDINE
24.	UTAH	RAUL LOPEZ	REAL MADRID (SPAIN)
25.	SACRAMENTO	GERALD WALLACE	ALABAMA
26.	PHILADELPHIA	SAMUEL DALEMBERT	SETON HALL
27.	VANCOUVER	JAMAAL TINSLEY	IOWA STATE
28.	SAN ANTONIO	TONY PARKER	PARIS BASKET RACING (FRANCE)

* MINNESOTA FORFEITED ITS FIRST-ROUND DRAFT SELECTION.

SAN ANTONIO SPURS STAR TONY PARKER'S NAME SHOWS UP OFTEN IN THE TOP ACCOMPLISHMENTS OF NBA PLAYERS 23 AND YOUNGER.

MOST PLAYOFF GAMES

PLAYER	GAMES
1. TONY PARKER	67
2. KOBE BRYANT	66
3. RICHARD JEFFERSON	40

MOST ASSISTS PLAYOFFS

PLAYER	ASSISTS
1. MAGIC JOHNSON	302
2. TONY PARKER	295
3. KOBE BRYANT	281

MOST POINTS PLAYOFFS

PLAYER	POINTS
1. KOBE BRYANT	1,264
2. TONY PARKER	1,087
3. MAGIC JOHNSON	587

SELFLESS. HARD

More money awaited him, and his playing time would have been limitless. After nine NBA seasons, no one would have blamed Brent Barry for selecting one of the long-term and more financially secure offers from either the Golden State Warriors or the Portland Trail Blazers last summer.

Five months shy of his 33rd birthday and with only 13 playoff games on his NBA résumé, the former three-point field goal percentage leader recognized the championship window might be closing on him. The opportunity to play for one of the most respected franchises, not only in the NBA, but in all of professional sports, and the ring was simply too great to pass up, even if it meant passing up more dollars.

"It's about having a chance to play for a team that's going to win and going to play the game the right way," Barry said. "I pride myself upon playing the game the right way. I think the things

I can do will be enhanced and give these guys an opportunity to get back where they want to be."

Where the Spurs wanted to be was the NBA Finals. After losing to the Los Angeles Lakers in the 2004 Western Conference Semifinals, where they missed 60 field goal attempts in Game 6, the case could be made that the Spurs wanted Barry and his ability to spread the defense as much as he wanted them.

As a longtime starter with the Seattle SuperSonics, Barry embraced his role coming off the bench with the Spurs even though the production wasn't quite up to his standards. In 81 games, the 6-foot-6-inch shooting guard averaged 21.5 minutes and 7.4 points. While his field-goal percentage hovered around 42 percent, well below his career average, that number spiked to 48.6 in the eight games he started.

Barry saved his best performance of the season for the most opportune time, the NBA Playoffs, when he scored 21 points, 13 in the fourth quarter, while dropping five three-pointers in Game 1 of the Western Conference Finals showdown between the Spurs and the Phoenix Suns.

"He came up huge," teammate Tony Parker said after the game. "I am very happy for him, because he's been struggling the whole season. He played great. I hope he's going to keep it going because we need him."

As much as Tim Duncan, Manu Ginobili and Parker grabbed the majority of headlines during the season, the Spurs' success didn't solely rest on the

WORKING. DETERMINED.

shoulders of their "Big Three." Rather, it also relied heavily — night in and night out — on the likes of Barry, Bruce Bowen, Robert Horry, Rasho Nesterovic, Nazr Mohammed, Beno Udrih and Devin Brown.

A point not lost on head Gregg Popovich.

"It's not about Parker or Duncan or Ginobili," Popovich said. "It's about team."

The team responded throughout the season. The Spurs bench was tested early and often. Seven games into the regular season, the visiting New York Knicks thought they had the chance to do the unthinkable, win a road game at the SBC Center. Holding Duncan to 17 points, the Knicks never had a chance as Parker notched 18, Barry and Bowen combined for 25, while Nesterovic chipped in with 10.

"You would think that if you can contain two out of the three best players [Duncan and Ginobili], you should have a chance," Knicks guard Jamal Crawford said.

The message to the Knicks and the rest of the NBA was quite clear: Duncan doesn't have to dominate for the Spurs to win. Not with the supporting cast highlighted by the likes of Bowen, one of the premier role players and defenders in the NBA. The 6-foot-7-inch forward, who wasn't drafted by an NBA franchise, played on seven teams — including two in France and two in the CBA — before finding a home in San Antonio. He became one of the key players in the Spurs pulling down the league's No. 1 defensive ranking.

Bowen earned All-NBA Defensive First Team honors for the second consecutive year, continuing to frustrate the league's premier scorers with suffocating, relentless, man-to-man defense.

"I take my defense very seriously," said Bowen, who also averaged career highs in points (8.2) and rebounds (3.5). "It's a dedication to hard work — doing the little things that won't get you the glory."

Another player who seeks championship hardware instead of stardom is Robert Horry. Statistics don't tell Horry's entire story, but his penchant for hitting big shots down the stretch in the biggest of games and his overall experience does.

"I'm just happy doing my role," Horry said. "I'm not going to try to be one of these players that step out and put a team on my back. I just like playing basketball and having fun with my guys."

He likes collecting championship rings, too. Horry arrived in San Antonio in 2003 in search of his sixth NBA championship. Not only did "Big Shot Rob"

complete his mission this season, he now joins Kareem Abdul-Jabbar, Michael Jordan and Scottie Pippen for the most NBA championships this side of Boston. Bill Russell reigns supreme with 11.

The Spurs' record of 59-23, which tied the Miami Heat for second-best in the NBA, is even more impressive considering that Tim Duncan missed 16 games while the Spurs went 9-7. The longest stretch was 12 beginning in late March. Rather than bemoan their fate, the Spurs rallied without the two-time NBA MVP.

"We've played without him before, and we just have to keep going," Parker said as the Spurs went 8-4 in Duncan's absence. "It's not like we have a choice. Our other big guys will have to do more, and the rest of us will have to step up."

One of those big guys is Mohammed, a mid-season acquisition who saw more and more playing time, when Duncan and Rasho Nesterovic went down with injuries, before eventually replacing the 7-foot Slovenian center in the starting lineup.

"He surpassed all of our immediate expectations," Popovich said. "His rebounding, his shot-blocking, his scoring have all been more than we expected and especially this quickly while he was trying to figure out the system and fit in.

"We would not be here [NBA Finals] without him. There's no doubt in my mind. He's really used his minutes wisely and helped us a great deal."

Once again, the Spurs pulled off another draft-day steal, courtesy of the superior talent evaluation skills of Popovich and the Spurs' General Manager R.C. Buford.

Beno Udrih, the 6-foot-3-inch point guard from Slovenia, may have been selected with the 28th overall pick in the 2004 NBA Draft, but he showed why he was a steal when he earned got milk? Western Conference Rookie of the Month honors for December. In 80 regular-season games, Udrih spelled Parker, averaging 14.4 minutes per game. He even netted a career-high 25 points in his first career start March 14 against the New Orleans Hornets.

Devin Brown, the 6-foot-5-inch guard, who broke out in the 2004 Western Conference Semifinals, hit his stride in late March, averaging 18 points over three games before being sidelined with a herniated disc. While forward Linton Johnson was injured most of the season, late-season acquisition Glenn Robinson along with Tony Massenburg and Sean Marks responded and contributed when called upon no matter the situation.

"Our guys have been great off the bench," Duncan said. "They are ready to come in — all the guys — on any given night."

THE SEASON

GREAT START, ALL-STAR ACCOLADES, HOME-COURT DOMINATION

San Antonio set the championship tone early. The Spurs inaugurated the 2004-05 season welcoming one of the NBA's elite teams — the Sacramento Kings — to the SBC Center on November 3. Unfortunately for the Kings, the Spurs weren't gracious hosts.

An aura of championship hope and optimism filtered through the arena that night. The Spurs were on a mission. The Los Angeles Lakers, the Spurs' playoff rival the last four years, were no longer a formidable foe with Shaquille O'Neal having taken his three NBA championships and 27-point and 12-rebound averages to Miami.

The Spurs wanted to reclaim their turf as the NBA's best team, and Tim Duncan, who finished a distant runner-up to Kevin Garnett in MVP voting the previous season, arrived ready to overthrow the incumbent in hopes of capturing his third such award.

Duncan shredded the Kings' front line, tallying 30 points and grabbing 14 rebounds, as the Spurs won their eighth straight opener, 101-85. In what would serve as a preview of things to come this season, Manu Ginoboli — fresh from leading Argentina to a gold medal at the Olympic Games in Athens, Greece — embraced the No. 2 scoring role and poured in 24 points in 28 minutes.

Although it was only one win, head coach Gregg Popovich liked what he saw.

"It was a good start to the new season," Popovich said. "We rebounded well. The defense was pretty good. It was better than fair."

The victory served as a springboard for the Spurs, who jumped out to a 8-1 start, the best franchise mark in 13 years. One of those victories, the November 12 home game versus O'Neal's Miami Heat, saw Popovich become the fifth-fastest coach in

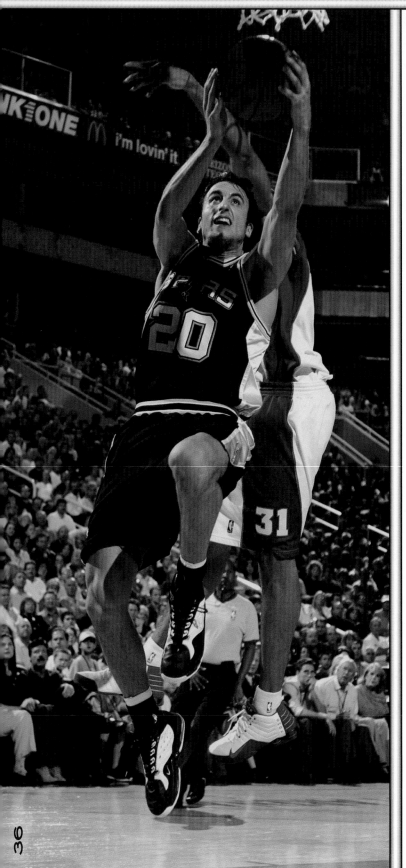

NBA history to notch 400 wins.

The Spurs entered December with the league's best record at 12-3, having won four in a row. During that streak, San Antonio won by no fewer than 14 points, holding the likes of Dallas (twice), Denver and Utah to less than 80 points.

The Spurs continued to set records, racing out to a 16-3 start, the best in franchise history, after defeating the Chicago Bulls 91-75 for their eighth victory in a row.

The Spurs were 62 seconds away from their 17th victory when Tracy McGrady of the Houston Rockets had other ideas. With eight wins in the first 19 games, the McGrady era was off to an underwhelming start. Down by 10 points and watching thousands of fans head for the exits, the Rockets staged a miraculous comeback, as the two-time NBA scoring champion exploded for 13 points in 35 seconds to give his team an improbable 81-80 victory.

"It was a great game, and we got sloppy at the end," Popovich said. "Tracy took advantage of it and was unbelievable. He's a great player."

The Spurs rebounded nicely from the unexpected loss, trouncing the Cleveland Cavaliers at home, 116-97. The team shot 84 percent from the field in the first half, breaking the previous franchise record of 78 percent, which was established against the New York Knicks on December 3, 1988.

The victories flowed as the Spurs defeated the New Orleans Hornets on December 17, to improve to 19-5.

San Antonio entered the New Year on a high note, grounding the high-octane Phoenix Suns — winners of 24 out of their first 27 games — to 94 points on 39.7 percent shooting.

"It was a huge game for us," Duncan said. "We shot the ball a lot better than they did. You don't want to say it's a statement game, but we were excited about the win."

Rookie Beno Udrih, the 28th pick out of Slovenia, ended up earning the got milk? Western Conference Rookie of the Month honors for December.

Bruce Bowen, one of the NBA's premier defensive players, lit it up on the offensive end when he scored a career high 24 points against the Lakers on his way to Western Conference Player of the Week honors in the first week of January. The Spurs continued to dominate at home, compiling a 20-1 mark after defeating the Washington Wizards on January 17 and running their record to 37-2 at the SBC Center since March 1, 2004.

After 41 games, the mid point of the NBA season, the Spurs owned the best record in the league at 32-9.

While the Suns were the talk of the NBA with the addition of Steve Nash and the improved play of Amaré Stoudemire, the Spurs once again made the strong case as to why they were the premier team in the Western Conference after defeating Phoenix for the second time. Ginobili scored a career-high 48 points, including 18 in the fourth quarter.

The Spurs, who annually go on the road every February for two weeks when the rodeo moves into the SBC Center, finished their trip 5-2 and tied Phoenix for the best record in the NBA at 41-12.

"We're not bad," Popovich said. "We've got a long way to go to compete for a championship. But, we're on the right track. And, we've got enough games left where if we focus and just pay attention, we can get better."

As the All-Star break approached, Popovich received the honor of coaching the Western Conference All-Stars, thanks to the Spurs' impressive first half. Despite two NBA championships and a NBA Coach of the Year Award on his résumé, it was surprisingly Popovich's first All-Star head coaching appearance.

"It is a great honor," Duncan said about the selection of Popovich as coach. In making his seventh All-Star Game appearance, Duncan joined Ginobili, who was making his first.

Four days after the All-Star Game, the Spurs said goodbye to one of the franchise's most popular players, Malik Rose, a valuable contributor on the 1999 and 2003 championship teams, and said hello to 6-foot-10-inch Nazr Mohammed.

The second half of the season wouldn't be so kind to the Spurs. Injuries plagued the team as the Spurs relinquished the best record in the NBA to the Suns. Duncan, who sprained his right ankle March 6 — the night the Spurs retired Sean Elliott's uniform No. 32 — would be placed on the injured list March 21 after re-aggravating it. The Spurs went without Ginobili for five games because of a groin injury and lost three straight, their longest losing stretch of the season.

San Antonio headed into the final month of the season without its two-time NBA MVP, Duncan, who ended up missing 12 games. The Spurs went 8-4 in his absence and added some extra scoring punch, signing free-agent forward Glenn Robinson. By the time Duncan returned to action April 13, the Spurs were still in the hunt for the best record in the league with Phoenix, but ultimately couldn't catch the Suns as San Antonio finished 3-3 in its remaining six games of the season. While the Spurs entered the postseason with a 38-3 home record — the best in franchise history — and captured their fourth straight division title, the road to the NBA Finals out West had to go through Phoenix.

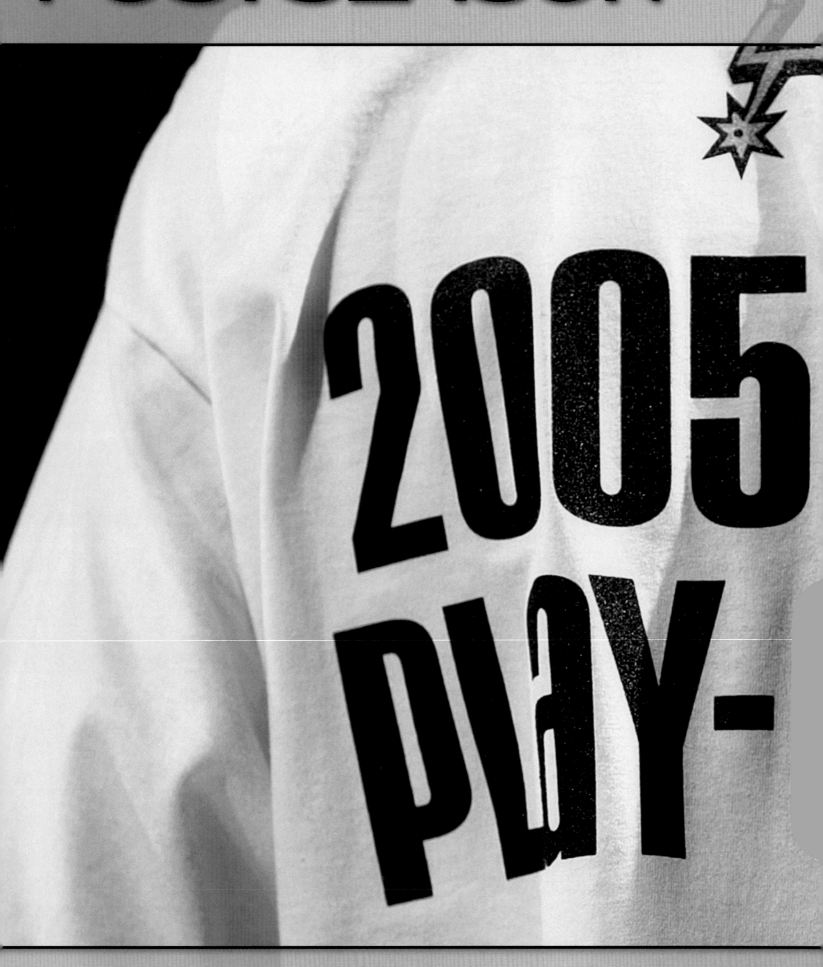

NBA PLAYOFFS

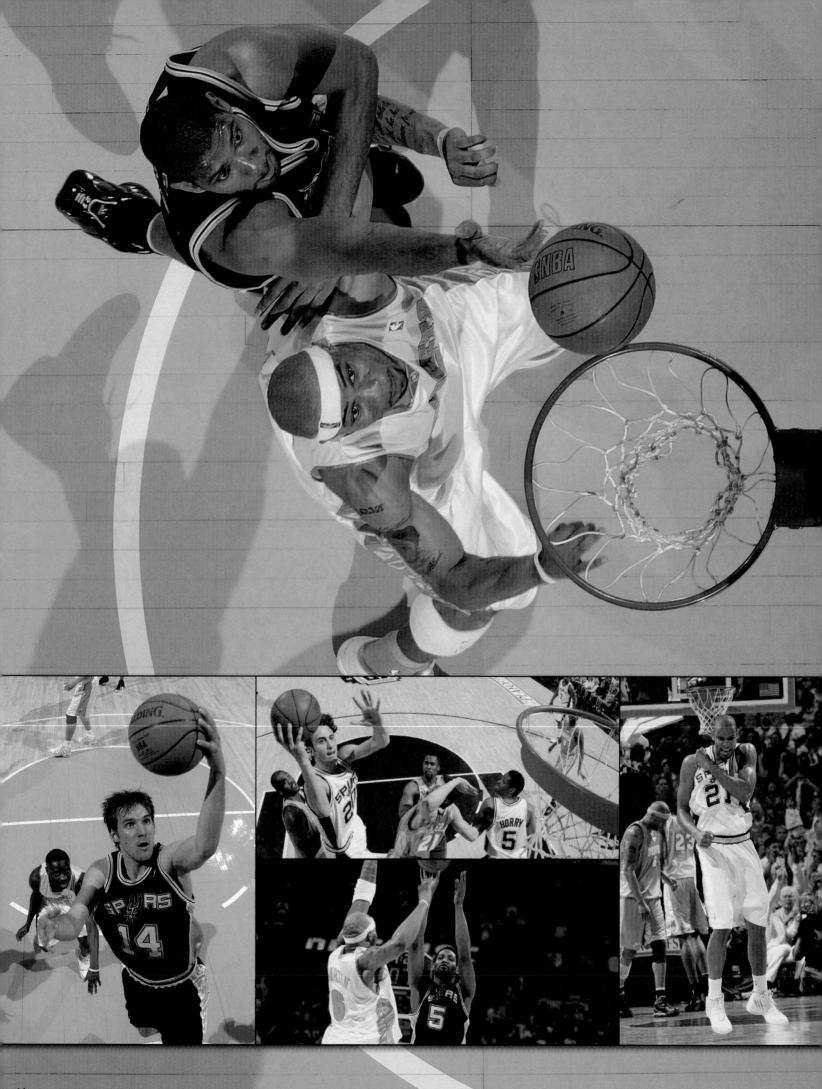

WESTERN CONFERENCE FIRST ROUND

GAME 1	NUGGETS 93	SPURS 87
GAME 2	SPURS 104	NUGGETS 76
GAME 3	SPURS 86	NUGGETS 78
GAME 4	SPURS 126	NUGGETS 115 (OT)
GAME 5	SPURS 99	NUGGETS 89

The quest for the NBA championship and the Larry O'Brien Trophy began with a thud. The Denver Nuggets, given new life and playing inspired basketball since George Karl took over for interim head coach Michael Cooper in January, did their best to spoil the Spurs' championship hopes and aspirations. The seventh-seeded Nuggets rolled into the first round boasting a 32-8 record under Karl and took a giant first step in pulling off the upset of the playoffs by defeating the heavily favored Spurs at the SBC Center in Game 1, 93-87.

Andre Miller scored 31 points for Denver, while Marcus Camby held Tim Duncan scoreless in the fourth quarter. While Denver's frontcourt blanketed Duncan for most of the game, it was apparent that the two-time NBA MVP was still feeling the effects of a sprained right ankle, which caused him to miss 12 games late in the season. With limited explosiveness, Duncan shot only 7-of-22 from the field, finishing with 18 points and 11 rebounds.

"I thought we benefited a little bit from Timmy being rusty," Nuggets coach George Karl said.

The win not only allowed the Nuggets to steal home-court advantage in the series, but sent a message to the rest of the league that they weren't going to lay down against a team with the second best record in the league.

"We felt confident," Camby said. "Everyone thought that the Spurs would run through us and everyone is talking about the Spurs vs. the Suns in the conference finals. This team has a lot of heart and a lot of pride."

Unfortunately for Camby and the Nuggets, their playoff victory total would end at one as the Spurs regained control of the series, winning Game 2 in a 28-point route, 104-76. Duncan scored 18 of his 24 points in the first half. Looking to gain some energy and rhythm from his bench, Spurs head coach Gregg Popovich replaced regular-season starter Manu Ginobili with Brent Barry, which paid big dividends.

The ultimate team player, Ginobili was eager to jumpstart the bench production, which he did, scoring 17, 32, 24 and 18 points in the following four games, all Spurs victories.

"We played a great team," Karl said. "We shook them in Game 1, but then they shook off the rust and got better after that."

 VS.

WESTEN CONFERENCE SEMIFINALS

GAME 1	SPURS 103	SUPERSONICS 81
GAME 2	SPURS 108	SUPERSONICS 91
GAME 3	SUPERSONICS 92	SPURS 91
GAME 4	SUPERSONICS 101	SPURS 89
GAME 5	SPURS 103	SUPERSONICS 90
GAME 6	SPURS 98	SUPERSONICS 96

Determined not to make the same mistake they did the previous round by losing the first game, the Spurs took care of business, jumping out to a 2-0 series lead against one of the NBA's most improved teams, the Seattle SuperSonics. Tony Parker and Tim Duncan starred in the Game 1 triumph, scoring 29 and 22 points, respectively, following up with 22 and 25, while super-sub Manu Ginobili added 28 in Game 2.

As Game 3 shifted to Seattle, few believed that the Sonics would have a chance to jump back in the series. Sonics head coach Nate McMillan was not one of them.

"They won the first two in San Antonio," McMillan said. "We go home now and we'll play in front of our home crowd. We still have an opportunity. They still have to win two more games. We'll make some adjustments again, and hopefully we'll get this thing right."

The Spurs appeared to be on the verge of taking a commanding 3-0 series lead when the free-throw roof caved in on them in the fourth quarter. The Spurs shot 8-of-16 from the line, and Ginobili, an 80 percent free-throw shooter, shockingly missed three of six attempts. Despite the collapse, the Spurs did have one final chance to win when Duncan's four-foot turn-around jumper bounced off the front of the rim as time expired, clinching the Sonics' victory, 92-91.

"Our performance at the free-throw line was a single-handed great way to lose a game," Spurs head coach Gregg Popovich said.

Inspired by the hometown fans, the Sonics responded in Game 4, thanks to Ray Allen's 32-point performance as the Spurs tumbled, 101-89, tying the series at two games each.

The pivotal Game 5 saw the re-emergence of Manu Ginobili in the starting lineup, leading the Spurs to victory, scoring a career playoff high 39 points and dishing six assists, while Bruce Bowen held Ray Allen to an 8-for-19 shooting performance en route to 19 points, four in the second half. The Spurs received a scare in Game 6 with Duncan re-injuring his left ankle injury with 8:08 remaining in the fourth quarter, but still managed to nail two critical free throws down the stretch to give his team a 78-77 lead. Allen bounced back from his Game 5 performance, scoring 25 points and barely missed sending the series to a seventh game when his three-pointer bounced off the rim as the final buzzer sounded. The Spurs won, 98-96, and were four wins away from their first NBA Finals appearance in two years.

 VS.

WESTERN CONFERENCE FINALS

GAME 1	SPURS 121	SUNS 114
GAME 2	SPURS 111	SUNS 108
GAME 3	SPURS 102	SUNS 92
GAME 4	SUNS 111	SPURS 106
GAME 5	SPURS 101	SUNS 95

It was the most highly anticipated series of the playoffs, featuring two of the premier teams out West. The Phoenix Suns owned the home-court advantage throughout the playoffs, thanks to the NBA best regular-season record of 62-20. The Suns also featured the highest scoring offense in the league in 10 years, averaging 110.4 points per game. The Spurs rolled to 58 victories while featuring the league's No. 1 defense, holding opponents to 88.4 per game. Something had to give, right?

"With Phoenix, we know it's going to be a faster game with more possessions, and we're ready to do that," Spurs head coach Gregg Popovich said.

It was the Spurs — not the Suns — who put on a scoring clinic in Game 1, beating Phoenix at its own game. The Spurs scored 43 points in the fourth quarter to win Game 1, 121-114. Brent Barry starred for San Antonio, scoring 13 of his 21 points in the fourth, including three three-pointers.

In Game 2, the fourth quarter once again proved to be magical for San Antonio, overcoming another deficit while flawlessly executing on the offensive end, this time posting 31 points on the board en route to 111-108 victory.

"The last two games, they have been phenomenal at making big shots in the fourth quarter," Suns point guard and NBA MVP Steve Nash said. "At some point, you've just got to congratulate them and say they are better than us."

The Suns, a team that yielded an average of 116 points to the Spurs in the first two games, were shut down in the first half of Game 3, scoring only 39 points, their lowest first-half total of the season. Even the reappearance of Phoenix guard Joe Johnson, who missed the six previous games with a fractured orbital bone, wasn't enough to lift Phoenix as the Spurs won, 102-92.

After three games in the series, the question wasn't which team was better, it was about whether the Suns could avoid the sweep. Phoenix responded in Game 4 as Amaré Stoudemire and Johnson took charge, scoring 31 and 26 points, respectively, as the Spurs went down at the SBC Center, 111-106.

Duncan made sure the Suns didn't get back in the series in Game 5, though, scoring 31 points and grabbing 15 rebounds, as the Spurs held Phoenix to 95 points. Stoudemire scored a playoff career high 42 points along with 16 rebounds capping off a sensational series for the 22-year-old in which he averaged 37 points for the five games.

Unfortunately for Suns fans, it wasn't enough to prevent the Spurs from making their second Finals appearance in three years.

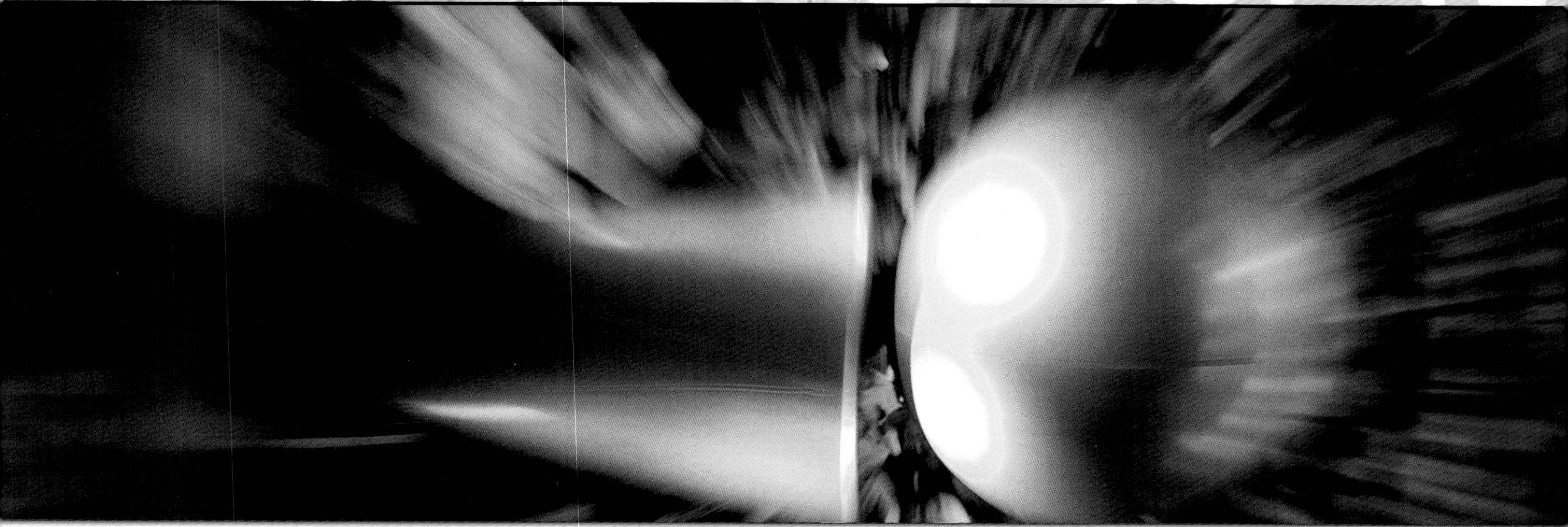

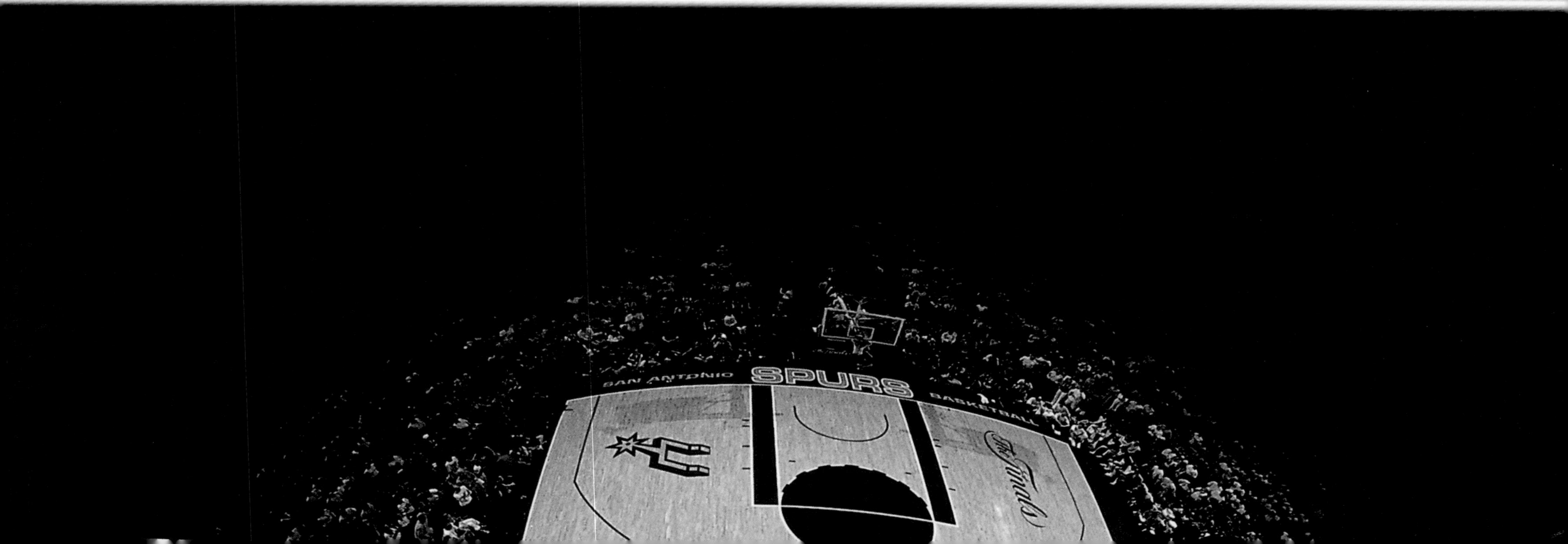
SAN ANTONIO
SPURS
BASKETBALL
The Finals

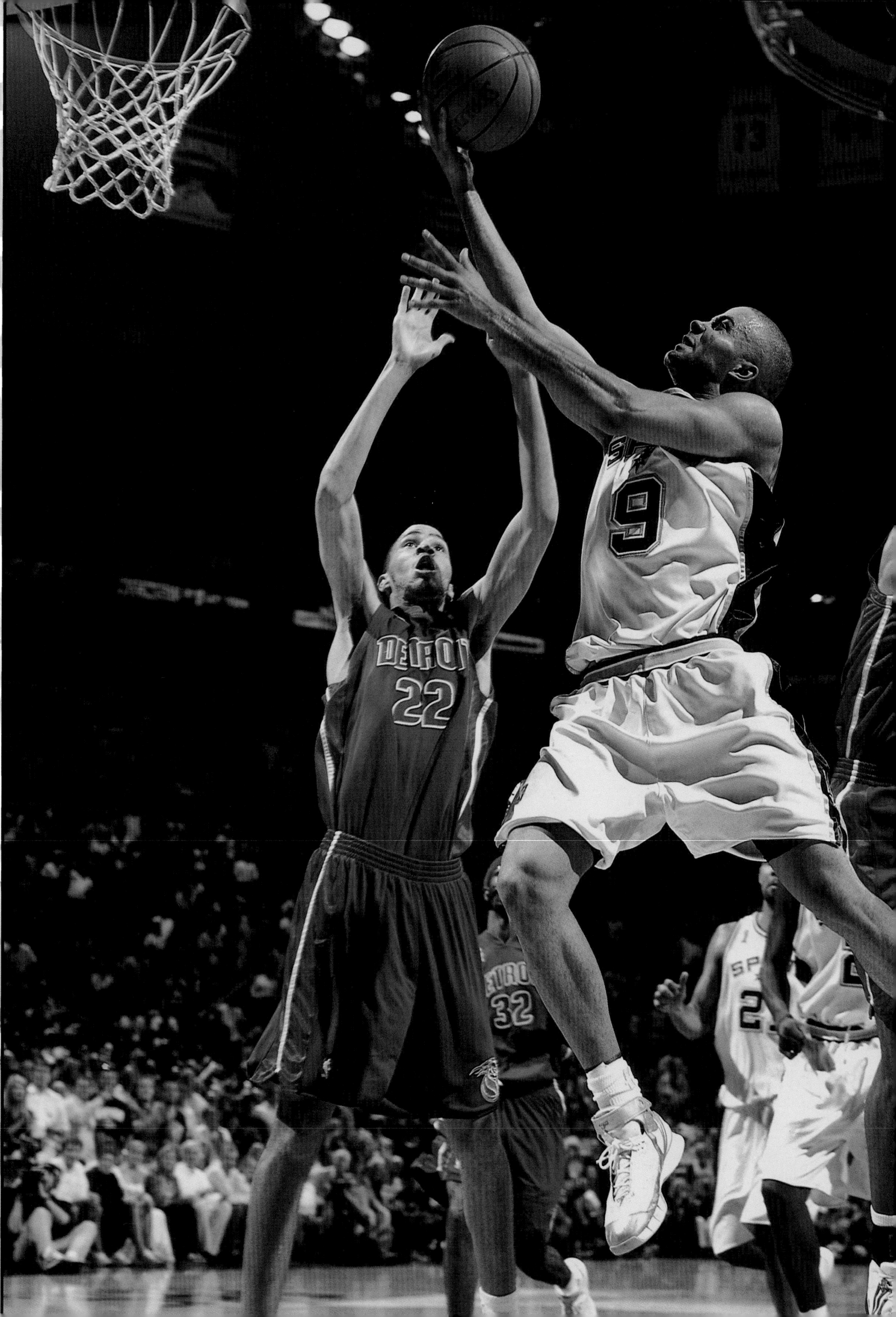
9
22
32

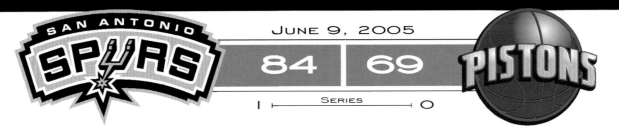

SAN ANTONIO SPURS

JUNE 9, 2005

84 | 69

PISTONS

I |—— SERIES ——| O

The storylines prior to Game 1 were in abundance. The matchup between the defending NBA champion Detroit Pistons and the San Antonio Spurs, their predecessor, presented plenty of intrigue and questions as the 59th NBA Finals were set to tip off.

It was the first time that the two previous champions met in the Finals since the Boston Celtics and Los Angeles Lakers clashed in 1987. Unlike that heated rivalry, mutual admiration between both sides was quite prevalent, beginning with Larry Brown and Gregg Popovich, whose friendship dates back to the 1972 Olympic men's basketball trials and has blossomed since. Brown took Popovich under his wing at the University of Kansas in 1986, and the star pupil credits a lot of his success to his mentor.

"I wouldn't be here without him," said Popovich who joined Brown as an assistant coach with the Spurs in 1988 and later was the best man at Brown's wedding. "He's had a huge impact on what I believe about the game, what wins and what loses — how to play the game."

What wins is defense, and Brown taught Popovich well. The Spurs

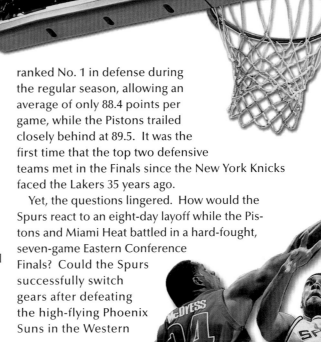

ranked No. 1 in defense during the regular season, allowing an average of only 88.4 points per game, while the Pistons trailed closely behind at 89.5. It was the first time that the top two defensive teams met in the Finals since the New York Knicks faced the Lakers 35 years ago.

Yet, the questions lingered. How would the Spurs react to an eight-day layoff while the Pistons and Miami Heat battled in a hard-fought, seven-game Eastern Conference Finals? Could the Spurs successfully switch gears after defeating the high-flying Phoenix Suns in the Western

" What it's about for us is **JUST PLAYING THAT 48-MINUTE GAME,** from start to finish. **"**

— Tim Duncan

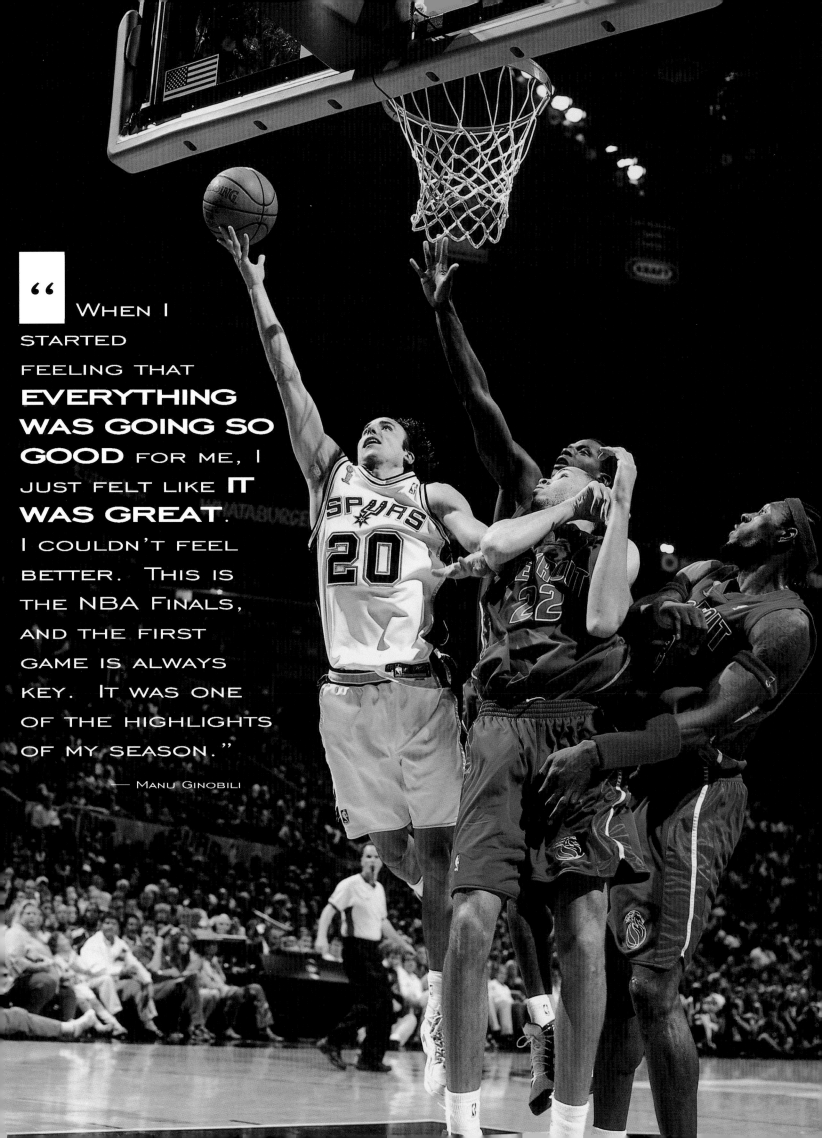

"WHEN I STARTED FEELING THAT **EVERYTHING WAS GOING SO GOOD** FOR ME, I JUST FELT LIKE **IT WAS GREAT**. I COULDN'T FEEL BETTER. THIS IS THE NBA FINALS, AND THE FIRST GAME IS ALWAYS KEY. IT WAS ONE OF THE HIGHLIGHTS OF MY SEASON."

— MANU GINOBILI

The Spurs are 3-0 all time in Game 1 of the NBA Finals.

Conference Finals and beat the Pistons at their own slow-down, half-court style of game? And, how would the Pistons respond only 48 hours after advancing to their second consecutive Finals appearance?

One of the answers appeared to present itself early, as the Spurs were feeling the effects of the layoff, turning the ball over four times in the first seven minutes and scoring only four points. The Pistons were clearly the aggressor, attacking the boards, blocking shots and keeping the Spurs off balance. Popovich went to his bench rotation early in the game, using a total of nine players, including Glenn Robinson, hoping to shake off the rust as the Spurs found themselves down 17-4 with a little less than five minutes remaining in the quarter.

When in doubt, go to the two-time NBA Finals MVP — and that's what San Antonio did, feeding the ball to Tim Duncan. The Spurs went on a 13-3 run to close the gap to three, trailing 20-17 at the end of the first quarter.

The Spurs continued to chip away at the lead, thanks to Duncan and the penetration abilities of Tony Parker, who routinely drove to the hoop. He attempted eight of his first nine shots and scored eight points in the last five minutes of the quarter.

As halftime approached, the Pistons were in a funk, except for Chauncey Billups, who scored 11 in the quarter. His teammates, Tayshaun Prince, who sat much of the quarter with two fouls, Ben Wallace, Rasheed Wallace and Richard Hamilton, all went scoreless in the period until Hamilton's basket with a minute remaining.

The defense and intensity picked up in the third quarter as the momentum continued to build for San Antonio. Duncan scored at the 8:45 mark to give the Spurs a 42-41 lead, their first since the opening moments of the game. The Spurs' defense stifled the Pistons, forcing them to miss 11 of 13 shots during one stretch as Bruce Bowen continued to blanket Hamilton, who missed five of six shots in the quarter.

Manu Ginobili, who was limited to four points on 1-for-6 shooting in the first half, took over in the fourth quarter, nominating himself as this year's candidate for the NBA's playoff slogan, "Where Legends Are Born." Ginobili sparked a 19-4 Spurs run, scoring 15 of his 26 points in the fourth. With off-balance shots, fall-aways and finger rolls, the Argentinean took Prince to school, dazzling the fans at the sold-out SBC Center, who remained on their feet during the Manu Ginobili Show. When the Pistons went on a 10-0 run to reduce the lead to seven, Ginobili continued his charge, driving into the lane for an emphatic one-handed dunk, nailing a three-pointer, and then a runner shortly after. His seven points in a little more than a minute iced the game for San Antonio.

"He was good, man," Billups said after the game. "He did what he does. He's a slasher. He can also shoot it. He's an energy guy. I thought he came out and did all of those."

The Finger Roll
Tim and Pop's Legacy

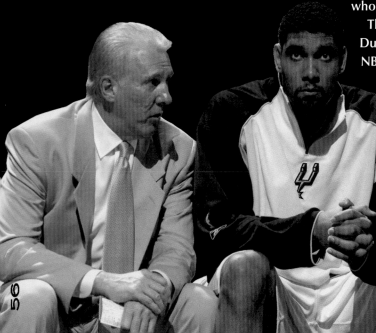

By George Gervin

As much as Tim Duncan and Gregg Popovich have accomplished in their respective NBA careers, there is still one elusive missing piece — winning an NBA title without "The Admiral," David Robinson. That would mean everything to those two.

Tim Duncan is a very special player, and everybody knows he can win the championship on his own. But, you still have to prove it. For Popovich, the challenge is to show the world that you have surrounded Duncan with players who are capable of bringing the title back to San Antonio.

The Spurs took a big step by winning Game 1 of the NBA Finals, and Duncan and "Pop" took a big one as well on their way to cementing their NBA legacies. Duncan has been nursing two sprained ankles throughout the playoffs and still managed to score 24 points, and grab 17 rebounds against the stingy interior defense of the Detroit Pistons.

As good as Duncan was, though, the star of the show was Manu Ginobili. He will give 100 percent, and, in Game 1, he really turned it on in the fourth quarter. He is so fundamentally sound. He can pass the ball, and he can score off the dribble, which is a rarity in today's game. Most guys need picks to get open and score, but Ginobili can slice down the middle without any help.

While Duncan may have lost The Admiral to retirement in 2003, he gained another premier Finals performer in 2005 in Ginobili.

San Antonio Spurs

Starters	POS	MIN	FGM-A	3PM-A	FTM-A	OF-R	DF-R	T-R	AST	STL	BLK	TO	PF	PTS
Bruce Bowen	SF	35	0-6	0-3	0-0	0	2	2	2	0	1	1	4	0
Tim Duncan	FC	41	10-22	0-0	4-5	6	11	17	2	0	2	3	2	24
Nazr Mohammed	C	26	4-8	0-0	2-2	4	3	7	0	1	2	0	1	10
Tony Parker	PG	41	7-17	0-1	1-2	1	3	4	3	0	0	4	1	15
Manu Ginobili	SG	39	10-16	2-4	4-4	3	6	9	2	1	0	4	3	26
Bench														
Robert Horry	PF	29	2-6	2-4	1-2	0	3	3	3	1	0	0	2	7
Brent Barry	G	9	0-1	0-1	0-0	0	1	1	0	0	0	1	4	0
Glenn Robinson	SF	6	1-2	0-0	0-0	0	3	3	0	0	3	0	0	2
Beno Udrih	PG	7	0-0	0-0	0-0	1	0	1	0	0	0	1	0	0
Devin Brown	SG	6	0-1	0-0	0-0	0	2	2	0	0	0	1	0	0
Rasho Nesterovic	C	1	0-0	0-0	0-0	0	0	0	0	0	0	0	0	0
Tony Massenburg	FC	DNP	Coach's Decision											
TOTALS			34-79	4-13	12-15	15	34	49	12	3	8	15	17	84
			43.0%	30.8%	80.0%				Team TO (points off): 16 (19)					

Pistons

Starters	POS	MIN	FGM-A	3PM-A	FTM-A	OF-R	DF-R	T-R	AST	STL	BLK	TO	PF	PTS
Tayshaun Prince	SF	32	4-12	0-0	3-4	2	3	5	4	1	0	3	2	11
Rasheed Wallace	FC	33	3-6	0-0	0-0	4	4	8	1	2	6	1	4	6
Ben Wallace	FC	39	2-5	0-0	1-2	1	6	7	1	2	3	1	3	5
Chauncey Billups	PG	43	9-16	1-4	6-6	0	4	4	6	4	1	1	1	25
Richard Hamilton	SG	39	7-21	0-1	0-1	1	0	1	1	0	0	2	2	14
Bench														
Antonio McDyess	PF	23	1-8	0-0	0-1	1	6	7	0	1	0	1	2	2
Lindsey Hunter	PG	16	1-5	0-1	0-0	2	1	3	1	1	0	2	3	2
Carlos Arroyo	PG	13	1-3	0-0	0-0	0	0	0	1	1	0	1	2	2
Darvin Ham	SF	1	1-1	0-0	0-0	0	0	0	0	0	0	0	0	2
Ronald Dupree	SF	1	0-0	0-0	0-0	0	0	0	0	0	0	0	0	0
Elden Campbell	FC	DNP	Coach's Decision											
Darko Milicic	FC	DNP	Coach's Decision											
TOTALS			29-77	1-6	10-14	11	24	35	15	12	10	12	19	69
			37.7%	16.7%	71.4%				Team TO (points off): 13 (15)					

" IT'S
ALWAYS FUN
WHEN SHOTS
ARE GOING
IN **FOR**
YOU."

— BRUCE BOWEN WHO
SCORED 15 POINTS
AND HIT 4-FOR-8 FROM
THREE-POINT RANGE
AFTER GOING SCORELESS
IN GAME 1.

SPURS
SIZZLE

GAME TWO

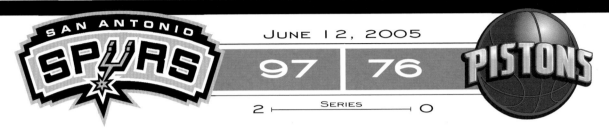

SAN ANTONIO SPURS

JUNE 12, 2005

97 | **76**

PISTONS

2 ⊢——— SERIES ———⊣ 0

Less than 48 hours after Game 1 ended, a sense of desperation set in for the Detroit Pistons. In the 58-year history of the NBA Finals, no defending champion had absorbed such a one-sided loss — 15 points — in the opener of the championship series. Game 2 was a must-win situation. After all, only two teams in NBA history have bounced back from 0-2 deficits — the 1969 Boston Celtics and the 1977 Portland Trail Blazers — to win the NBA title. The Pistons would have preferred not to be the third.

It was redemption time for last season's champions. Surely Rasheed Wallace would attempt more than five field goals, or Ben Wallace would reach double figures in rebounds. Tayshaun Prince and Richard Hamilton definitely would shoot better than a combined 11-for-33 from the field, right?

The opportunity to fly out of San Antonio with a split and head to Detroit was within reach for the Pistons, no matter how disastrous Game 1 appeared to be. It was a new day, a new game.

Thirteen seconds into Game 2 — in front of an audience of 115 million television viewers around the world — those thoughts quickly vanished.

Manu Ginobili — 24-foot three — good! … Tony Parker's running-jumper … good! … *Bruce Bowen — 23-foot three from the corner — good!* One minute and 31 seconds into the game, the Pistons trailed 8-0 as 18,797-plus delirious fans in San Antonio's SBC Center smelled a rout. At the

TWO-GAME
LEAD

8:33 mark of the first quarter, the Spurs were up, 11-2.

Ginobili continued to dazzle, picking up where he left off in Game 1. Whether he was running a flawless give-and-go with Parker or penetrating the lane and drawing two defenders before whipping the ball to Robert Horry for an uncontested three-pointer, the Argentinean once again was proving to be the difference-maker.

Horry was everywhere in the first half, diving for loose balls, grabbing rebounds, amassing nine points, three steals, three assists and four rebounds in 14 minutes of action.

The horrid shooting for Detroit continued as Chauncey Billups, Richard Hamilton and Tayshaun Prince were a combined three-of-15 from the field for seven points.

Misses on nine shots within four to six feet of the basket compounded Detroit's problems. If Antonio McDyess hadn't provided a 12-point lift off the bench, the 58-42 halftime deficit would have been much worse.

Chants of "Go Spurs Go!" grew louder by the second in the third quarter as Billups and Hamilton combined for 10 points, while the Pistons managed to match the Spurs' point total in the period with 21.

The Pistons made their move in the fourth quarter, going on a 10-0 run while reducing the Spurs' lead to eight, 81-73, with 7:13 remaining. Down by as many as 23 at one point in the game, the Pistons now had new life as the Spurs called timeout. Hopes of further whittling the lead vanished when Ginobili took control, nailing two free throws after Rasheed Wallace committed his fifth foul. When Beno Udrih hit two more from the stripe, the lead increased to 15, thanks to a Ginobili steal, which led to Bowen's fourth three-pointer of the game.

"Every time we chipped away at it," Chauncey Billups said, "they hit us with another [blow]."

Chants of "MVP! MVP! MVP!" rang throughout the arena when Ginobili stepped up to the free throw line, putting the finishing touches on his 27-point, seven-assist performance while outscoring his defender Tayshaun Prince by 24 points.

When the final buzzer sounded, the Spurs had a 97-76 victory and a two-game lead in the Finals as the stat crews were still assessing the Pistons' wreckage. Since Detroit's sprint to a 17-4 lead in Game 1, the Spurs' defense clamped down and San Antonio outscored the defending champions by 49 points through Game 2.

"Right now, with the way they're playing and executing, and the contributions they're getting from a lot of people, they've just dominated two ball games," Detroit head coach Larry Brown said, looking forward to a return to Detroit for Game 3. "Hopefully, with our crowd, we'll come out throwing the first punch and being aggressive, and we'll see."

The Finger Roll
Bowen Gets Offensive

By George Gervin

Once again, Bruce Bowen did the job on the defensive end, frustrating Richard Hamilton into back-to-back 14-point performances. In two games, Hamilton shot 12 of 36 from the field, and Bowen is a big reason why.

What probably surprised a lot of people was Bowen's offensive assertiveness and output in Game 2. Bowen scored 15 points, including four 3-pointers while attempting eight for the game. Overall, Bowen attempted 13 shots, three more than Tim Duncan. When was the last time that happened?

When Bowen gets on a roll like that, the Spurs are especially difficult to beat. After Game 1, when Bowen went scoreless, a lot was said about his offensive limitations and how he only excelled on the defensive end. I think he put that to rest by letting his overall game do his talking. Even when he went scoreless in Game 1, Larry Brown called him the most dominant player on the floor for the first three quarters, which is quite a compliment.

There isn't any doubt that Bowen sets the tone for the Spurs' No. 1 ranked defense, and his teammates and coaches appreciate his intensity and work ethic on a nightly basis. But, when teams dare him to shoot, like the Pistons did in Game 2, he'll make them pay.

SAN ANTONIO SPURS

Starters	POS	MIN	FGM-A	3PM-A	FTM-A	OF-R	DF-R	T-R	AST	STL	BLK	TO	PF	PTS
Bruce Bowen	SF	36	5-13	4-8	1-2	0	3	3	1	1	0	1	3	15
Tim Duncan	FC	37	5-10	0-0	8-9	3	8	11	1	0	4	2	2	18
Nazr Mohammed	C	25	1-2	0-0	4-5	3	2	5	0	0	2	2	2	6
Tony Parker	PG	28	6-9	0-1	0-1	0	1	1	2	0	0	0	5	12
Manu Ginobili	SG	32	6-8	4-5	11-13	1	2	3	7	3	0	3	3	27
Bench														
Brent Barry	G	26	0-3	0-3	0-0	0	1	1	5	2	0	2	1	0
Robert Horry	PF	28	4-10	2-6	2-2	1	5	6	5	4	1	2	2	12
Beno Udrih	PG	18	2-4	1-1	2-2	0	2	2	2	1	0	2	0	7
Glenn Robinson	SF	3	0-1	0-0	0-0	0	0	0	0	0	0	1	0	0
Rasho Nesterovic	C	3	0-0	0-0	0-0	1	2	3	0	0	0	0	0	0
Devin Brown	SG	2	0-0	0-0	0-0	0	0	0	0	0	0	0	1	0
Tony Massenburg	FC	2	0-2	0-0	0-0	0	1	1	0	0	0	0	0	0
TOTALS			29-62	11-24	28-34	9	27	36	23	11	7	15	19	97
			46.8%	45.8%	82.4%				Team TO (pts off): 16 (14)					

PISTONS

Starters	POS	MIN	FGM-A	3PM-A	FTM-A	OF-R	DF-R	T-R	AST	STL	BLK	TO	PF	PTS
Tayshaun Prince	SF	33	1-7	0-0	1-1	1	2	3	0	0	1	1	4	3
Rasheed Wallace	FC	33	5-12	0-2	1-2	3	5	8	4	2	0	1	5	11
Ben Wallace	FC	33	4-6	0-0	1-3	4	4	8	2	0	1	3	3	9
Chauncey Billups	PG	40	6-14	0-3	1-1	1	4	5	3	0	0	4	3	13
Richard Hamilton	SG	35	5-15	0-0	4-5	2	5	7	3	1	0	0	4	14
Bench														
Lindsey Hunter	PG	24	3-7	0-1	1-2	2	2	4	3	1	0	1	1	7
Antonio McDyess	PF	24	7-14	0-0	1-2	3	4	7	2	1	0	2	4	15
Carlos Arroyo	PG	8	2-3	0-0	0-0	0	1	1	0	0	0	1	1	4
Darvin Ham	SF	4	0-1	0-0	0-0	2	0	2	0	0	0	0	0	0
Ronald Dupree	SF	3	0-2	0-0	0-0	0	0	0	0	0	0	0	0	0
Darko Milicic	FC	3	0-1	0-0	0-0	0	0	0	0	0	0	0	0	0
Elden Campbell	C	DNP Coach's Decision												
TOTALS			33-82	0-6	10-16	18	27	45	17	5	2	13	25	76
			40.2%	0.0%	62.5%				Team TO (pts off): 14 (13)					

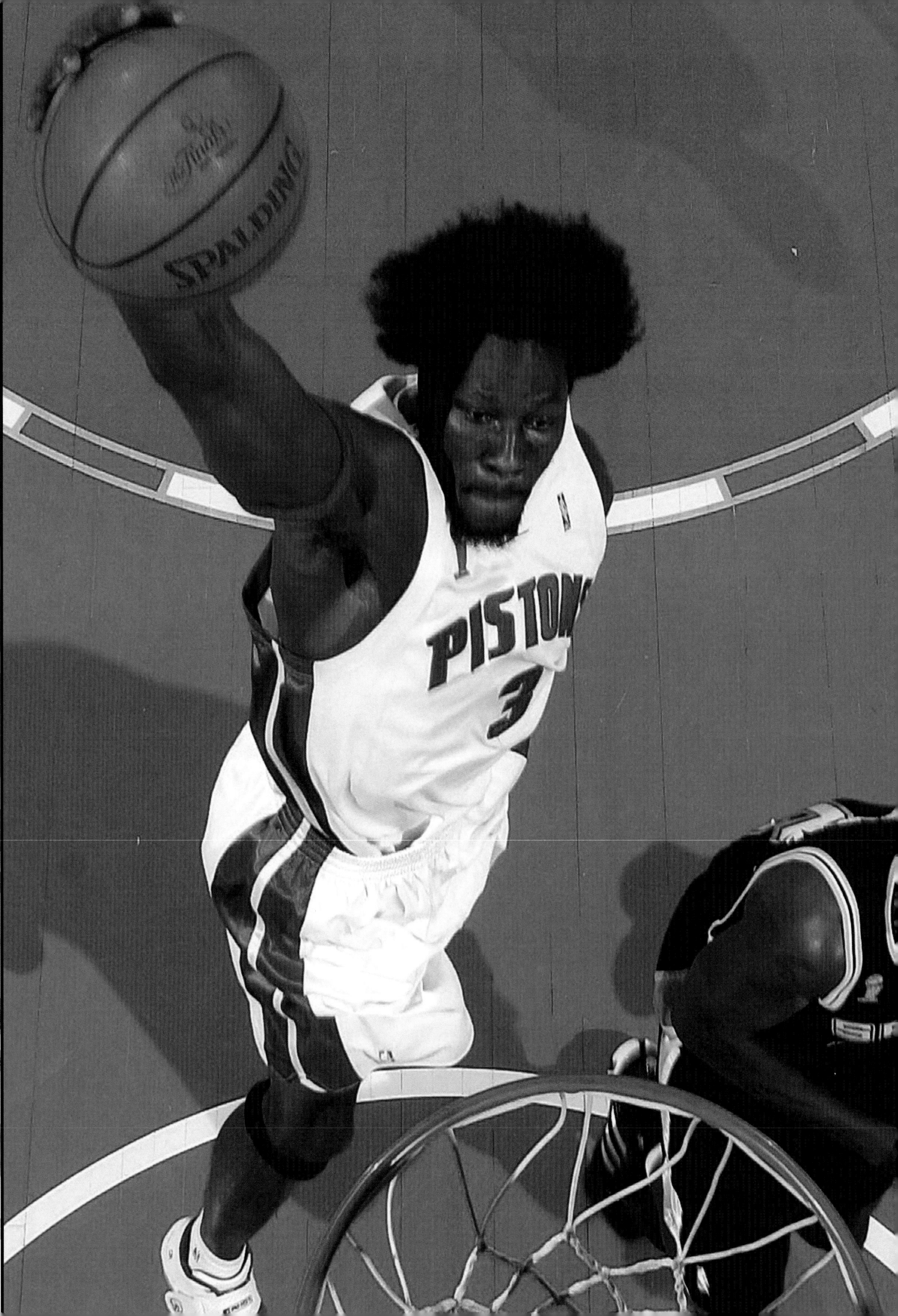
SPALDING
3

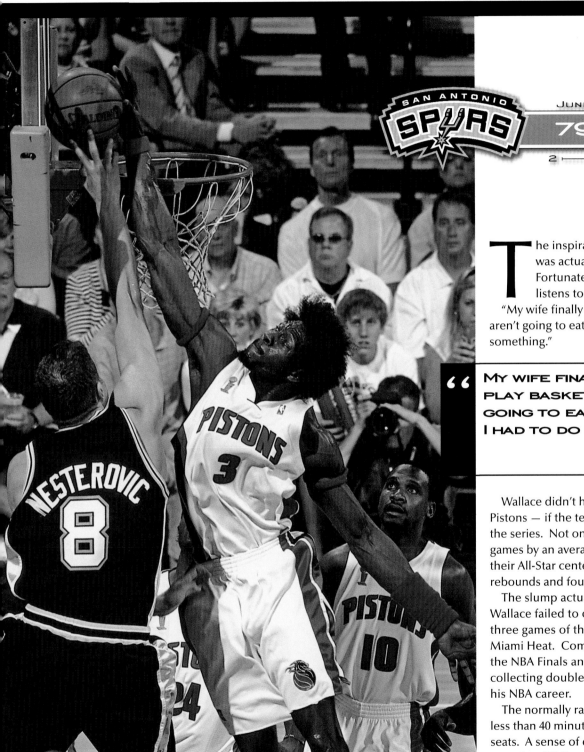

SAN ANTONIO SPURS **79** | **96** **PISTONS**

JUNE 14, 2005

SERIES 2 —————— 1

T he inspiration came from an unlikely source. It was actually more of a directive than anything. Fortunately for the Detroit Pistons, Ben Wallace listens to his wife.

"My wife finally just told me 'go play basketball, or you aren't going to eat [when you get home].' I had to do something."

> **" MY WIFE FINALLY JUST TOLD ME 'GO PLAY BASKETBALL, OR YOU AREN'T GOING TO EAT (WHEN YOU GET HOME).' I HAD TO DO SOMETHING."**
>
> — BEN WALLACE,
> PISTONS CENTER

Wallace didn't have a choice — and neither did the Pistons — if the team had any hope of jumping back into the series. Not only did the Pistons lose the first two games by an average of 17 points, but the production from their All-Star center was un-Wallace-like compiling 15 rebounds and four blocked shots in 72 minutes.

The slump actually began before the NBA Finals, when Wallace failed to collect 10 or more rebounds in the last three games of the Eastern Conference Finals against the Miami Heat. Combine that with the first two games of the NBA Finals and "Big Ben" went five games without collecting double figures, the longest playoff drought of his NBA career.

The normally raucous Palace crowd was rather subdued less than 40 minutes before the tip-off as fans filed to their seats. A sense of despair had set in. The Pistons needed a spark — Wallace's energy, intimidation, aggressiveness provided all that and then some only two seconds into the game. He stole Manu Ginobili's inbound pass and

BIG BEN
INSPIRES PISTONS

proceeded to race down court to deliver an emphatic dunk, one that also served as a declaration to the sold-out crowd.

Yes, Wallace was back — and so were the Pistons.

Big Ben was everywhere in the first quarter, blocking Tim Duncan's first shot attempt on his way to five for the period along with three steals, six offensive rebounds and seven points. Wallace set the tone and the Pistons responded.

"Ben was great from the first play," Pistons teammate Richard Hamilton said. "He was unbelievable. He brought a lot of energy. It was important, because we

> " **BEN WAS GREAT FROM THE FIRST PLAY. HE WAS UNBELIEVEABLE.**"
> — RICHARD HAMILTON,
> PISTONS GUARD

didn't let them hit us first and react to that. We took it to them."

The Spurs received a setback less than 30 seconds into the game when Ginobili collided with Tayshaun Prince and suffered a thigh bruise. It was evident that Ginobili wasn't going to be his same whirling-dervish self when he returned more than four minutes later. His stat line reflected as much, because he finished the night with seven points, no assists, four rebounds and five turnovers.

It was also a forgettable performance for Ginobili's teammate, Tim Duncan. The two-time NBA Finals MVP suffered one of his worst Finals performances as Wallace and the Pistons' defense denied him the ball and prevented him from establishing a presence in the post. Duncan missed 10 of 15 shots and finished with 14 points.

"Ben was great," Duncan said about Wallace. "He came out with a lot of energy and really got the crowd and his team into it."

In the third quarter, Wallace continued to inspire when he was on the receiving end of a Hamilton alley-oop pass, slamming home a back-to-the-basket, over-the-head dunk that sent the fans into a frenzy. While the Spurs managed to tie the game at 63 with 1:36 remaining in the third quarter, the Pistons took over the rest of the way, outscoring San Antonio 33-16.

Hamilton broke out of his shooting slump with 24 points, and Billups finished with 20 points — but, the night belonged to Wallace. The Palace favorite ended up with his first double-double of the 2005 NBA Finals, finishing with 15 points, 11 rebounds, five blocked shots and three steals.

"That's the Ben Wallace we all know and love," Billups said. "There's no one like him in the league. He's the best at what he does. Ben Wallace won the game. He really did." 🏀

By George Gervin

The Finger Roll

Pistons Motoring at The Palace

The Pistons were happy to be home, and they sure played like it, feeding off the sell-out crowd at The Palace. The Pistons' leader by example, Ben Wallace, set the tone on the opening play and his teammates followed his lead, playing the Detroit Pistons' style of basketball — hard work, hard fouls, hustle and plenty of determination.

This did not look like the team that was blown out of Games 1 and 2 in San Antonio. The Pistons played with a lot of confidence and were the aggressors from the opening tip.

The collision between Spurs' forward Manu Ginobili and Pistons' forward Tayshaun Prince in the first quarter had a lasting impact on the Spurs. Ginobili was not the same player when he returned from the bench after bruising his thigh. His effectiveness was limited, and he didn't play with the same fearlessness that we were accustomed to seeing.

A big problem for the Spurs was foul trouble. Head coach Gregg Popovich had to try a few different lineup combinations. He brought in Rasho Nesterovic, who really has not played in the postseason. The foul trouble also forced him to go with Brent Barry early. He had to mix up his lineup, and that put pressure on the team. But, the Detroit Pistons deserve a lot of credit for forcing the Spurs to go to their bench early and deal with a different rotation.

The Pistons played with a lot of hunger and desire. Richard Hamilton bounced back from two subpar games, while Chauncey Billups played well and the team received a boost from the bench with Antonio McDyess. This was a big confidence builder for the Pistons. Detroit did what they are supposed to do, win on their home court.

As ballplayers, we figure that we might have one or two bad games. This was one for the Spurs, but give the Pistons credit. At the end of Game 3, one thing became clear: The Spurs need to win one game in Detroit or the pressure would be back on them.

SAN ANTONIO SPURS

STARTERS	POS	MIN	FGM-A	3PM-A	FTM-A	OF-R	DF-R	T-R	AST	STL	BLK	TO	PF	PTS
Bruce Bowen	SF	36	5-13	4-8	1-2	0	3	3	1	1	0	1	3	15
Tim Duncan	FC	37	5-10	0-0	8-9	3	8	11	1	0	4	2	2	18
Nazr Mohammed	C	25	1-2	0-0	4-5	3	2	5	0	0	2	2	2	6
Tony Parker	PG	28	6-9	0-1	0-1	0	1	1	2	0	0	0	5	12
Manu Ginobili	SG	32	6-8	4-5	11-13	1	2	3	7	3	0	3	3	27
BENCH														
Brent Barry	G	26	0-3	0-3	0-0	0	1	1	5	2	0	2	1	0
Robert Horry	PF	28	4-10	2-6	2-2	1	5	6	5	4	1	2	2	12
Beno Udrih	PG	18	2-4	1-1	2-2	0	2	2	2	1	0	2	0	7
Glenn Robinson	SF	3	0-1	0-0	0-0	0	0	0	0	0	0	1	0	0
Rasho Nesterovic	C	3	0-0	0-0	0-0	1	2	3	0	0	0	0	0	0
Devin Brown	SG	2	0-0	0-0	0-0	0	0	0	0	0	0	0	1	0
Tony Massenburg	FC	2	0-2	0-0	0-0	0	1	1	0	0	0	0	0	0
TOTALS			29-62	11-24	28-34	9	27	36	23	11	7	15	19	97
			46.8%	45.8%	82.4%				Team TO (pts off): 16 (14)					

PISTONS

Starters	POS	MIN	FGM-A	3PM-A	FTM-A	OF-R	DF-R	T-R	AST	STL	BLK	TO	PF	PTS
Tayshaun Prince	SF	33	1-7	0-0	1-1	1	2	3	0	0	1	1	4	3
Rasheed Wallace	FC	33	5-12	0-2	1-2	3	5	8	4	2	0	1	5	11
Ben Wallace	FC	33	4-6	0-0	1-3	4	4	8	2	0	1	3	3	9
Chauncey Billups	PG	40	6-14	0-3	1-1	1	4	5	3	0	0	4	3	13
Richard Hamilton	SG	35	5-15	0-0	4-5	2	5	7	3	1	0	0	4	14
BENCH														
Lindsey Hunter	PG	24	3-7	0-1	1-2	2	2	4	3	1	0	1	1	7
Antonio McDyess	PF	24	7-14	0-0	1-2	3	4	7	2	1	0	2	4	15
Carlos Arroyo	PG	8	2-3	0-0	0-0	0	1	1	0	0	0	1	1	4
Darvin Ham	SF	4	0-1	0-0	0-0	2	0	2	0	0	0	0	0	0
Ronald Dupree	SF	3	0-2	0-0	0-0	0	0	0	0	0	0	0	0	0
Darko Milicic	FC	3	0-1	0-0	0-0	0	0	0	0	0	0	0	0	0
Elden Campbell	C	DNP Coach's Decision												
TOTALS			33-82	0-6	10-16	18	27	45	17	5	2	13	25	76
			40.2%	0.0%	62.5%				Team TO (pts off): 14 (13)					

PISTONS' INTENSITY SEIZES
SERIES

GAME FOUR

SAN ANTONIO SPURS June 16, 2005 **102 | 71** **PISTONS**

2 —— SERIES —— 2

The San Antonio Spurs had 48 hours to shake off their Game 3 disappointment.

The NBA's best defensive team, which had never given up 90 points in 13 Finals' games, had surrendered 96 to the Detroit Pistons.

So, the question hovering over the two-time NBA champions before tip-off hung in the air like a last-second shot: Which Spurs' team was going to show up for Game 4? Would it be the one that picked the Pistons apart in Games 1 and 2 with flawless precision and execution on the offensive and defensive ends, or the team that looked out of sorts and overwhelmed in Game 3?

It took all of two seconds to gain a sense of what kind of night was in store for San Antonio when Manu Ginobili picked up a personal foul a few seconds after the opening tip.

The Pistons, who embraced the role of the aggressor in Game 3 — not like the team on its heels to open the series — continued with the full throttle, relentless pressure, forcing the Spurs into five turnovers in their first 11 possessions.

The Pistons were in constant transition, pressing, trapping and frustrating the Spurs while seamlessly parading to the basket

Richard Hamilton, dunk … Ben Wallace, layup … Ben Wallace, another layup … Rasheed Wallace, jumper… Chauncey Billups, driving layup …

The dribble penetration by Tony Parker, which was so effective in the first two games, nearly disappeared as a wall of Piston defenders anticipated each drive.

The Pistons ran off 11 consecutive points to begin the second quarter, thanks to their bench, which was much maligned before the Finals began, as Lindsey Hunter and Antonio McDyess led the way. The Spurs continued to sputter on offense, missing their first six shots and

DOMINANCE

going scoreless until 8:04 of the quarter when Devin Brown drained a three-pointer.

It was a forgettable first half for the Spurs, who trailed 51-36, shooting only 35.5 percent and netting only one more field goal than turnover, 11-10.

The fans at The Palace, with their noise-making Thunderstix, were in full force in the third quarter as the Pistons' bench continued to sparkle. Hunter, who heated up with four jumpers and a free throw in three minutes, led the way with nine points. The Pistons continued to pour it on in the fourth quarter highlighted by a rare Hunter dunk that brought the house down with 2:26 remaining in the game. It was a quarter in which the Pistons outscored the Spurs 28-14 en route to a 31-point win, 102-71, to even the series at two games each.

> " IT WAS A REALLY UGLY LOSS. THERE WAS NOT MINUTE IN THE WHOLE GAME THAT WE WERE CLOSE."
>
> — SPURS GUARD MANU GINOBILI,
> WHO FINISHED WITH 12 POINTS
> AND THREE ASSISTS IN 32 MINUTES

What was especially discouraging for San Antonio was the second straight lackluster performance from Tim Duncan. The two-time NBA MVP missed 12 of 17 shots as both Wallaces — Ben and Rasheed — continued to frustrate him with blanketing defense.

"It's a very physical game," said Duncan, who was held to five points in the second half. "Those guys throw a lot of bodies into you, and each with their own little style. Some are physical, some are loose or whatever it may be."

After 48 minutes, the Pistons not only took control of the series, they left the Spurs wondering what hit them. Seven Pistons finished with double figures in points, highlighted by the production from the bench. Hunter and McDyess finished with 17 and 13 points, respectively, while the defense produced 13 steals compared to one for the Spurs. Detroit also forced 18 Spurs turnovers, which led to 25 points while only coughing it up a Finals record low four times. It was what Pistons head coach Larry Brown called a perfect game.

"I really believe, in all honesty, that this is probably the best game a team that I've been involved with, in such an important game, it's the best game that we've played," Brown said.

For the Spurs, Game 4 played out a lot like Game 3, unable to match the Pistons' intensity while not heeding their coach's advice in "valuing the ball."

Did the Spurs lack the killer instinct? Shades of last season's collapse against the Los Angeles Lakers after being up 2-0 in the Western Conference Finals only to lose the next four now hovered over the team.

"This was a carbon copy of Game 3," Spurs head coach Gregg Popovich said. "It's disappointing that their physical play and defense have taken away everything we tried to do. We didn't learn anything from the last game. If it doesn't get any better, we'll be in big trouble."

By George Gervin

The Finger Roll
We Have a Series

Detroit played their brand of hard-nosed basketball and shut Manu Ginobili and Tim Duncan down. The Pistons are rough, tough and physical.

Ginobli scored 57 points the first two games. The next two, he had a total of 19. He and Tony Parker got knocked down every time they went to the hole. In effect, the Pistons said, "You got off on us in San Antonio. But, we are going to knock you down a few times and see if you are really tough enough."

Tim Duncan wasn't as aggressive as he needed to be and admitted as much. He needed to do a little more on the offensive end. With Ben Wallace and Rasheed Wallace taking turns guarding him, Ben is going to beat him up, and Rasheed is bigger and longer. Tim must go up strong and try to get to the foul line.

You have to hope that the Spurs can respond in Game 5. If you lose three in a row, you start having doubts. It does shatter your confidence. We all know confidence is hard to gain, but easy to lose. With how things are going, Detroit has to have the confidence that they can sweep the Spurs at home. But, until someone loses on their home court, San Antonio has that advantage. If you think about it, Detroit was really just catching up. Game 5 will be the pivotal one. San Antonio has to make a statement and prove that those first two games were not a fluke.

This is the kind of series we all envisioned: The two top teams in the league are playing a chess match out there. But, neither team has the king yet.

I like this series. This is where champions are born.

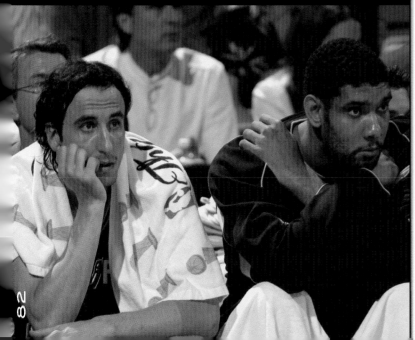

SAN ANTONIO SPURS

STARTERS	POS	MIN	FGM-A	3PM-A	FTM-A	OF-R	DF-R	T-R	AST	STL	BLK	TO	PF	PTS
Bruce Bowen	SF	33	2-3	0-0	2-2	1	2	3	4	0	2	3	4	6
Tim Duncan	FC	39	5-17	0-0	6-9	3	13	16	2	0	3	3	2	16
Nazr Mohammed	C	17	2-6	0-0	0-0	3	2	5	0	0	0	1	2	4
Manu Ginobili	SG	32	4-9	1-5	3-4	0	4	4	3	1	1	2	3	12
Tony Parker	PG	37	6-13	0-1	0-2	0	4	4	4	0	1	3	2	12
Bench														
Brent Barry	G	11	1-2	1-2	0-0	1	0	1	0	0	0	1	2	3
Robert Horry	PF	20	2-6	1-3	0-0	3	1	4	0	0	1	1	1	5
Beno Udrih	PG	11	2-5	1-2	0-0	0	0	0	0	0	0	2	2	5
Devin Brown	SG	20	2-8	1-2	3-5	1	2	3	2	0	0	0	1	8
Rasho Nesterovic	C	14	0-0	0-0	0-2	0	2	2	0	0	1	1	1	0
Tony Massenburg	FC	6	0-1	0-0	0-0	0	2	2	0	0	0	0	1	0
Glenn Robinson	SF	DNP Coach's Decision												
TOTALS			26-70	5-15	14-24	12	32	44	15	1	9	17	21	71
			37.1%	33.3%	58.3%				Team TO (pts off): 18 (25)					

PISTONS

Starters	POS	MIN	FGM-A	3PM-A	FTM-A	OF-R	DF-R	T-R	AST	STL	BLK	TO	PF	PTS
Tayshaun Prince	SF	36	6-14	0-2	1-1	2	0	2	1	2	0	0	2	13
Rasheed Wallace	FC	33	6-10	2-2	0-1	2	6	8	2	2	2	0	3	14
Ben Wallace	FC	39	5-11	0-0	1-4	5	8	13	1	3	3	0	3	11
Richard Hamilton	SG	38	4-16	0-1	4-4	2	7	9	4	1	0	1	4	12
Chauncey Billups	PG	38	5-14	0-4	7-7	0	5	5	7	2	0	1	1	17
BENCH														
Lindsey Hunter	PG	22	7-10	0-0	3-3	0	1	1	5	2	0	0	4	17
Antonio McDyess	PF	19	6-11	0-0	1-1	2	5	7	1	1	1	1	4	13
Carlos Arroyo	PG	7	1-3	0-0	1-2	0	0	0	2	0	0	0	0	3
Darvin Ham	SF	4	0-0	0-0	0-0	0	0	0	0	0	0	0	1	0
Ronald Dupree	SF	2	0-0	0-0	0-0	0	0	0	0	0	0	0	0	0
Darko Milicic	FC	2	1-1	0-0	0-0	0	2	2	0	0	0	0	0	2
Elden Campbell	C	DNP Coach's Decison												
TOTALS			41-90	2-9	18-23	13	34	47	23	13	6	3	22	102
			45.6%	22.2%	78.3%				Team TO (pts off): 4 (6)					

BIG GAME. BIG TIME.

SAN ANTONIO SPURS **96** | **95** **PISTONS**

JUNE 19, 2005

3 —— SERIES —— 2

A legacy appeared to lie in the balance. In a matter of 72 hours, the San Antonio Spurs were reeling. A once commanding 2-0 series lead evaporated as quickly as Tony Parker's first step, and so did the control of the series, not to mention the psychological edge.

After Games 3 and 4 at The Palace in Auburn Hills, Michigan, in which the Spurs lost by an average of 21 points, it was now open season on the two-time NBA champions and, specifically, their leader Tim Duncan. One of the premier players of his generation, Duncan, who has made the Finals his personal showcase by winning two NBA Finals MVP awards, had yet to get on track on the road. Unable to gain his customary position under the boards, thanks to the bruising rotating coverage of Ben and Rasheed Wallace, the numbers were subpar by Duncan's standards — 10 of 32 from the field for 30 points in two games, while even being outscored by Pistons' reserve guard Lindsey Hunter in Game 4, 17-16.

Columnists and broadcasters covering the Finals questioned Duncan's passion, along with his desire to combat aggression with aggression, along with his team's ability to win in Detroit. Even Duncan's former teammate, Sean Elliott, called No. 21's Game 3 performance the worst of his playoff career.

It was unchartered waters for Duncan, who — along with his coach and teammates — had roughly 72 hours to move beyond their 31-point drubbing in Game 4 and win in arguably the most hostile home arena in the NBA. With a chance to close out the series back in San Antonio in Game 6 as incentive, it was a daunting challenge — one that Duncan embraced on the eve of Game 5.

"I am the leader of this team," Duncan said. "So, it starts with me, and I understand that."

So did the Spurs, who went to their leader early and often in Game 6 as Duncan led the Spurs in points and rebounds in the first quarter with eight and six. Not only did the Spurs control the boards in the first half, but the Parker-Duncan-Manu Ginobili triumvirate was back, scoring 33 of the team's 42 first-half points.

BIG SHOT ROB,

A series highlighted by blowouts in each of the first four games featured a tie at halftime. The pressure mounted in the second half, as both teams realized what was at stake. In the previous 23 occasions a Finals was tied 2-2, the Game 5 winner had gone on to win the title 17 times. After getting poor percentage looks at the basket for much of the third quarter, the Pistons finished strong, ripping off an 11-2 run before Robert Horry scored his first points of the game by nailing a three-pointer with one second remaining.

Nine seconds into the fourth quarter, Horry was at it again, hitting another three-pointer, giving the Spurs a four-point lead. Horry, who surpassed Michael Jordan for the record for most made three-pointers in NBA Finals history in Game 3 with his 43rd, added to his tally.

With the Spurs down three with 3:47 remaining in the fourth quarter — Boom! A 25-foot shot to tie the game at 79.

Whenever the Pistons responded, whether it was Richard Hamilton, Rasheed Wallace or Chauncey Billups, Horry answered with free throws, tip-ins or more threes, including another 25-footer with 1:16 remaining that quickly turned the Pistons' two-point lead into a Spurs advantage.

Billups, known to his teammates as "Mr. Big Shot," carried the Pistons down the stretch, drove to the basket and scored with 51 seconds left to give the Pistons a one-point

> " **IT WAS PROBABLY THE GREATEST PERFORMANCE I'VE EVER BEEN A PART OF. HE WAS SO CALM. PUT HIM IN A BIG GAME IN THE FOURTH QUARTER, AND HE SHOWS UP. HE'S 'BIG SHOT ROB.'"**
> — TIM DUNCAN
> ON ROBERT HORRY'S PERFORMANCE

lead. Duncan, who struggled from the free-throw line in the fourth quarter, missed all six attempts before converting one with 33.8 seconds remaining to tie the game at 89.

The frustration would continue for Duncan when he missed a golden opportunity to win the game in the closing seconds, but couldn't slam home a rebound of Ginobili's running layup that rolled off the rim and into his hands.

"YOU'RE UP TWO WITH NINE SECONDS TO GO, THE ONLY THING YOU'RE THINKING IS: NO THREE-POINT SHOT. NO EXPLANATION. ULTIMATELY, IT'S ON ME. WE TALKED ABOUT WHAT WE WANTED TO DO, BUT THE GUY MADE A GREAT SHOT."

— LARRY BROWN

In overtime, the Pistons jumped out to a four-point lead before Horry decided to add to his personal highlight reel. He faked his defender, Tayshaun Prince, to the left on the free-throw line and soared to the hoop before throwing down a left-handed dunk while getting fouled by Richard Hamilton. That cut the lead to two points. Then, Duncan, who hadn't scored a field goal in the last nine minutes, uncharacteristically let a pass from Horry slip through his hands on the Spurs' next possession. Prince quickly retrieved the ball as the Pistons looked to add to their lead.

When Chauncey Billups missed a layup, Duncan scooped the rebound and quickly called time out. With 9.4 seconds remaining in the game, the Spurs had a final opportunity — and Horry had a chance to cement his legend as one of the NBA's greatest playoff clutch performers.

Horry inbounded the ball to a cutting Ginobili, who drew the attention of Rasheed Wallace, who made the mistake of leaving "Big Shot Rob" open. Horry took a pass right back from Ginobili and rattled in a three-pointer to give the Spurs a one-point lead as 22,076 Detroit fans stood stunned. The Pistons called time out and drew up a play for Hamilton, who missed badly on his attempt at a driving runner just inside the foul line as Parker blanketed him.

In a game that featured 18 ties and 12 lead changes, the Spurs were flying to San Antonio with a 3-2 series advantage, thanks in large part to Horry, the man with five NBA championship rings. Big Shot Rob came off the bench and scored 21 of his team's final 35 points. Eighteen of Horry's 21 points came in the fourth quarter and overtime as he converted five three-pointers in the second half. It was yet another spectacular performance by Horry, who had performed similar clutch heroics for the Houston Rockets and Los Angeles Lakers.

"That's what he does," Spurs head coach Gregg Popovich said. "He was unbelievable."

Horry's mesmerizing play in the Game 5 classic not only positioned the Spurs to clinch their third title in seven years, it also relieved Duncan, who, despite finishing with 26 points and 19 rebounds, had faltered down the stretch.

"He pulled me out of an incredible hole that I put myself in."

By George Gervin

The Finger Roll

Big Shot Rob's Classic Performance

The Spurs accomplished their goal: Win at least one in Detroit before heading back to San Antonio.

It was a big win for the Spurs and, on the flip side, a big loss for Detroit. This was a game the Pistons needed to keep the Spurs on their heels. Tim Duncan bounced back from two tough games, and he was awesome. He was a lot more aggressive and he seemed determined to stay in the paint — he also hit some big jump-hooks.

That got everybody off to a good start. He was definitely having some problems from the free-throw line. Free throws are all about confidence, and you can tell he kind of lost some in the fourth quarter. I know Duncan can make free throws because he broke my franchise record when he made 15 in a row.

As much as Duncan stepped up for the Spurs throughout the game, the real star of the show was Robert Horry. He did not score in the first half, but he came through when the Spurs needed him the most. After the game, when asked where his performance ranked all time in Finals history, Horry said probably around 25th or so.

He was being much too modest. His Game 5 performance ranks on the short list of the greatest ever. There are very few people who can do what he does. He has five championships with two different teams, and he has hit some of the biggest shots in playoff history with the Rockets, Lakers, and now the Spurs. He has an amazing amount of confidence in his game.

Detroit played as well as they could and they can't be counted out. This is a team that is known for coming back from deficits. But, they have not won in San Antonio in eight years and that has to be in the back of their minds. San Antonio has some of the best fans in basketball and the Pistons will be coming into the lion's den in Game 6. It will be tough for them to see a Game 7.

SAN ANTONIO SPURS

	POS	MIN	FGM-A	3PM-A	FTM-A	OF-R	DF-R	T-R	AST	STL	BLK	TO	PF	PTS
Bruce Bowen	SF	44	4-8	2-5	0-0	0	5	5	3	1	0	3	4	10
Tim Duncan	FC	48	11-24	0-0	4-11	8	11	19	2	0	2	2	3	26
Nazr Mohammed	C	26	3-4	0-0	0-0	1	2	3	0	1	0	0	3	6
Manu Ginobili	SG	44	5-16	0-4	5-5	3	3	6	9	1	0	2	4	15
Tony Parker	PG	45	7-15	0-3	0-0	1	1	2	3	0	0	6	4	14
Bench														
Brent Barry	G	22	1-3	1-2	0-0	1	1	2	0	0	1	0	3	3
Robert Horry	PF	32	7-12	5-6	2-3	5	2	7	2	0	0	3	5	21
Devin Brown	SG	4	0-0	0-0	1-2	0	1	1	1	0	0	0	0	1
Tony Massenburg	FC	DNP Coach's Decision												
Glenn Robinson	SF	DNP Coach's Decision												
Rasho Nesterovic	C	DNP Coach's Decision												
Beno Udrih	PG	DNP Coach's Decision												
TOTALS			38-82	8-20	12-21	19	26	45	20	3	3	16	26	96
			46.3%	40.0%	57.1%			Team TO (pts off): 17 (16)						

PISTONS

STARTERS	POS	MIN	FGM-A	3PM-A	FTM-A	OF-R	DF-R	T-R	AST	STL	BLK	TO	PF	PTS
Tayshaun Prince	SF	48	5-10	0-1	0-0	3	6	9	3	3	1	1	3	10
Rasheed Wallace	FC	41	6-15	0-0	0-0	1	4	5	1	3	4	0	5	12
Ben Wallace	FC	48	4-9	0-0	5-6	5	7	12	1	0	4	2	1	13
Richard Hamilton	SG	49	7-15	0-0	1-2	1	3	4	2	0	0	5	5	15
Chauncey Billups	PG	44	11-26	2-7	10-11	3	2	5	7	0	0	1	2	34
Bench														
Antonio McDyess	PF	17	4-6	0-0	1-2	3	3	6	1	0	2	1	3	9
Lindsey Hunter	PG	18	0-3	0-1	2-2	0	1	1	2	1	0	1	1	2
Elden Campbell	C	DNP Coach's Decision												
Darvin Ham	SF	DNP Coach's Decision												
Carlos Arroyo	PG	DNP Coach's Decision												
Ronald Dupree	SF	DNP Coach's Decision												
Darko Milicic	FC	DNP Coach's Decision												
TOTALS			37-84	2-9	19-23	16	26	42	17	7	11	11	20	95
			44.0%	22.2%	82.6%			Team TO (pts off): 12 (16)						

ALL ACCESS PASS 2005
Detroit
The Finals

DEEE-TROIT BASKETBALL

RICK

Spurs 55 TOL 4:1 6:46 PER 3 TOL 4:1 Pistons 55

GAME SIX

JUNE 21, 2005

| SPURS | 86 | 95 | PISTONS |

3 ———— SERIES ———— 3

The celebration began around 3:30 Monday morning when the Spurs' charter flight touched down at San Antonio International Airport. About 5,000 fans gathered — dressed in silver and black — waving "Go Spurs Go" signs and cheering deliriously as their heroes exited the plane one by one.

It was only hours ago that the balance of the NBA Finals tilted in the Spurs' favor thanks to the new "Prince of San Antonio," Robert Horry, who delivered one of the greatest clutch performances in championship series history.

Momentum and fate were smiling on the Spurs, who owned a 3-2 series lead with Game 6 to be played at the comforts of cozy SBC Center, a place where the home team lost only three times during the regular season. The Spurs had escaped Detroit with the one victory they needed. It was time to take their place in NBA history.

The champagne was on ice and the Spurs' championship victory plans were under way. The fiesta-style blowout was not lost on the Detroit Pistons, who love to crash such parties. It was familiar territory for Detroit, who not only respond in elimination game scenarios, but thrive in them.

Game 6 was the fifth time in 13 months that the Pistons faced a win-or-go-home situation. Although the Pistons rolled to a perfect 4-0 record in the previous games, a little extra motivation never hurt. Seven words — all underlined — would appear at the top of the chalkboard in the Pistons' locker room before Tuesday night's Game 6.

"San Antonio's Parade Is Scheduled for Thursday!!!"

The parade would have to be postponed because the Pistons came out firing in Game 6. Chauncey Billups and Richard Hamilton combined for three three-pointers in the first

NOT DONE. NOT YET.

quarter, only five less than the team made the entire series. The Spurs also were feeling it from long range, nailing three as well, courtesy of Manu Ginobili, Brent Barry and Bruce Bowen. The nip-and-tuck first half featured 18 lead changes and five Pistons' three-pointers as the Spurs' lead teetered on a single point, 47-46.

Billups and Hamilton continued their hot shooting in the third quarter, combining for 19 of the Pistons' 25 points to take a 71-67 lead into the fourth.

Plagued by foul trouble, Rasheed Wallace picked up his fifth with 11:23 to play in the game. Relegated to cheering his teammates from the bench, Wallace returned to action at the 5:18 mark and quickly atoned for his self-admitted "bonehead play" in leaving Horry open to hit the game-winning three in Game 5. Wallace nailed a 14-foot baseline jumper and followed that up with a three-pointer from the corner, ultimately scoring seven of the Pistons' nine points in the remaining 4:28.

Defensively, Wallace also came up with a few gems, including stripping the ball from Ginobili. While Wallace excelled down the stretch for Detroit, the Spurs faltered, failing to score after Tim Duncan's basket with 2:22 remaining, which gave San Antonio an 87-86 lead. Detroit outscored San Antonio 8-0 down the stretch as the Spurs went zero for their last seven possessions.

While Ginobili and Parker seemed to penetrate at will in the first half, the second half wasn't as kind with the Pistons' defense clogging the middle, forcing the Spurs to shoot from the perimeter. Ginobili was only two-for-eight from three-point territory for the game and had an uncharacteristically un-Ginobili-like finish, committing a turnover, having his shot blocked by Ben Wallace and hoisting two rushed three-pointers.

"I didn't have the same energy as in the first half," Ginobili said, "but, still, I think that even with the energy

that I had available I could have done a way better job making decisions in the last five minutes. Even though it's not the same energy, I am still very upset because of the way I played down the stretch."

While the Spurs struggled from the free-throw line, converting only 16 of 26 attempts, they also attempted a franchise record 28 three-pointers, converting only eight. The Pistons nailed eight of 17 with Billups' five leading the way.

"That's definitely too many," Spurs head coach Gregg Popovich said about his team's number of three-point attempts. "A lot of those were hurried. It was a matter of trying to win quickly, skipping steps."

For the Pistons, it was another demonstration of their resiliency, the championship resolve that pushed their record to a perfect 5-0 in elimination games as the series shifted to a dramatic Game 7.

"This is what our team is about," Pistons head coach Larry Brown said. "I kept fielding that question about how we could get ourselves ready to play again. I've been with these guys for two years, and they don't disappoint me in terms of their desire to win."

By George Gervin

The Finger Roll
Championship Resolve

The Detroit Pistons showed once again why they never can be counted out. Many wondered how the Pistons would respond from the Game 5 overtime loss, especially coming down to San Antonio in a hostile arena. The Pistons appeared unfazed — they embraced their role as underdogs and responded with a victory.

Detroit placed a lot of pressure on San Antonio, and this made it hard for them to execute their game plan. The Spurs could not come up with that big play to get them over the hump down the stretch. The Pistons rode the hot three-point shooting of Chauncey Billups, while Richard Hamilton and Rasheed Wallace provided the clutch baskets when the game was in flux. I thought Larry Brown also came up huge when in the huddle late in the game he told his players, "Hey guys, I forgot to tell you something. I love you guys." That is important. The players went out there and they wanted to win for their coach.

The Spurs' stars have to step up and prove that they are legends of the game. You can play well, win awards and go to All-Star Games, but, to be a true legend, you have to be consistent on the biggest stage. We have not seen this from San Antonio. Brent Barry was the only solid player for them in Game 6. Tony Parker turned the ball over and Manu Ginobili got a little reckless down the stretch.

Tim Duncan has also been struggling. The Pistons are doing their best to make it difficult for him to score. But, the beautiful part about it is that he still has another game to come through and win the series. I have a lot of confidence in "Big Tim," and I know he can play. But, he is going to have to hit some free throws. He has to get his confidence back to when he made 15 in a row against Phoenix in Game 3 of the Western Conference Finals.

Game 7 is all about the will to win. The San Antonio Spurs have proven they are champs and I just have this feeling that they will pull it out.

SAN ANTONIO SPURS

STARTERS	POS	MIN	FGM-A	3PM-A	FTM-A	OF-R	DF-R	T-R	AST	STL	BLK	TO	PF	PTS
Tayshaun Prince	F	44	5-10	0-2	3-4	3	4	7	4	1	1	0	3	13
Rasheed Wallace	F	24	7-15	2-5	0-1	1	2	3	3	2	3	1	5	16
Ben Wallace	C	44	4-6	0-0	0-2	3	6	9	0	2	3	0	2	8
Chauncey Billips	G	39	6-16	5-9	4-4	2	4	6	6	0	0	0	4	21
Richard Hamilton	G	44	9-19	1-1	4-5	1	4	5	3	0	0	2	0	23
BENCH														
Lindsey Hunter	PG	16	2-3	0-0	0-0	1	1	2	2	1	0	0	3	4
Antonio McDyess	PF	28	4-10	0-0	2-3	2	6	8	1	0	1	2	4	10
Carlos Arroyo	PG	1	0-0	0-0	0-0	0	0	0	0	0	0	0	0	0
Elden Campbell	C	DNP	Coach's Decision											
Darvin Ham	SF	DNP	Coach's Decision											
Ronald Dupree	SF	DNP	Coach's Decision											
Darko Milicic	FC	DNP	Coach's Decision											
TOTALS			37-79	8-17	13-19	13	27	40	19	6	8	5	21	95
			46.8%	47.1%	68.4%				Team TO (pts off): 5 (6)					

PISTONS

STARTERS	POS	MIN	FGM-A	3PM-A	FTM-A	OF-R	DF-R	T-R	AST	STL	BLK	TO	PF	PTS
Bruce Bowen	SF	41	2-8	2-6	0-0	0	2	2	1	0	0	1	2	6
Tim Duncan	FC	40	8-14	0-0	5-10	5	10	15	1	0	1	0	2	21
Nazr Mohammed	C	24	1-3	0-0	2-2	5	3	8	0	0	0	1	1	4
Tony Parker	PG	38	7-15	1-3	0-1	0	2	2	5	0	0	4	4	15
Manu Ginobili	SG	41	7-17	2-8	5-8	1	9	10	3	2	0	3	3	21
BENCH														
Brent Barry	G	25	3-10	1-5	4-5	1	1	2	3	0	0	1	2	11
Robert Horry	PF	30	3-6	2-5	0-0	1	3	4	2	1	1	1	4	8
Beno Udrih	PG	1	0-2	0-1	0-0	0	0	0	0	0	0	0	0	0
Tony Massenburg	FC	DNP	Coach's Decision											
Greg Robinson	SF	DNP	Coach's Decision											
Rasho Nesterovic	C	DNP	Coach's Decision											
Devin Brown	SG	DNP	Coach's Decision											
TOTALS			31-75	8-28	16-26	13	30	43	15	3	2	11	18	86
			41.3%	28.6%	61.5%				Team TO (pts off): 12 (14)					

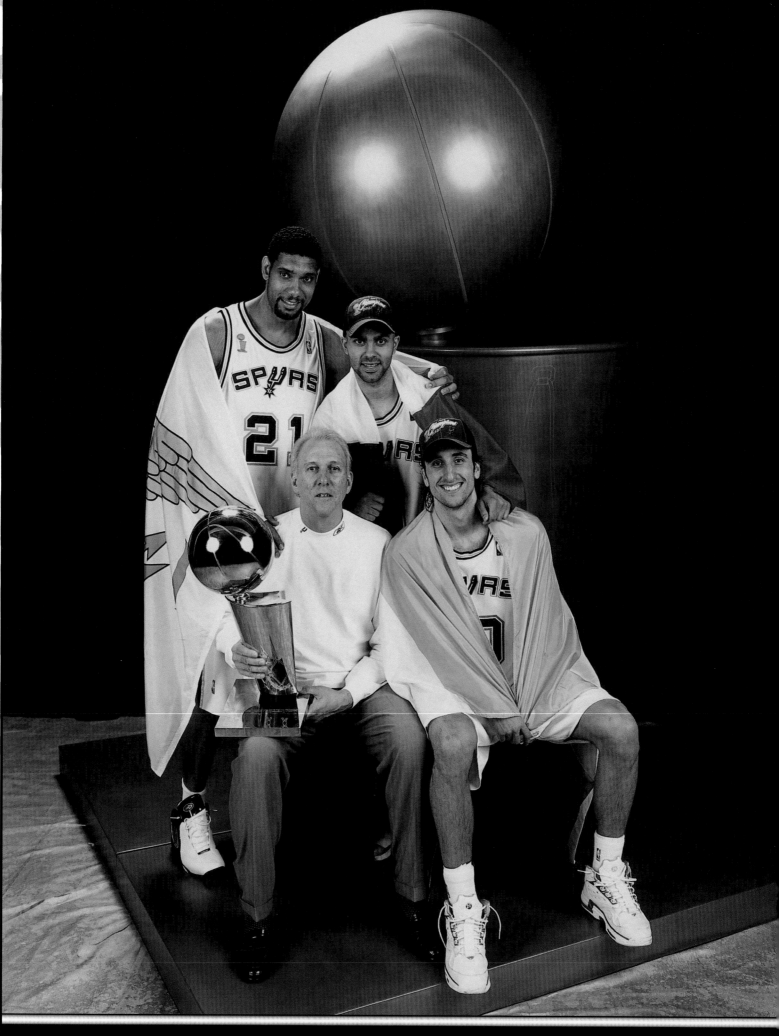

ONE TEAM. ONE GOAL.

GAME SEVEN

SAN ANTONIO SPURS

JUNE 23, 2005

SPURS 81 | 74 **PISTONS**

4 ←——— SERIES ———→ 3

San Antonio was a city on edge, holding its collective breath for what appeared to be an eternity until the first Game 7 of the NBA Finals since 1994 tipped off. The biggest sporting event in the history of the city loomed and the pressure built inside and outside the SBC Center.

A new kind of jitters fluttered among the Spurs' faithful and their favorite players. Going the distance in any playoff round, let alone the NBA Finals, marked unfamiliar territory for the San Antonio Spurs and the fans. The last time the Spurs advanced to a seventh game of the playoffs was in 1990, when the Portland Trail Blazers defeated them in the Western Conference Finals. Only 48 minutes separated the Spurs and Detroit Pistons from holding the coveted Larry O'Brien Trophy.

"Of course, you're nervous, a little anxious because whatever you did in the last 10 months, it comes back to just one game," Spurs forward Manu Ginobili said.

The Pistons not only regained the momentum, but found their swagger as well. On the brink of elimination in Game 6 and needing to win in a place where they haven't done so since 1997, the Pistons not only liked their chances, but also felt they were destined to win in this insurmountable odds fashion.

The Pistons didn't have time for the talk that no team has ever come back from a 3-2 deficit on the road since the Finals went to a 2-3-2 format in 1985. The Pistons also didn't have any time to discuss the fact that no team has won back-to-back Game 7's during the same postseason as a visitor, a feat they hoped to accomplish since defeating the Heat in Game 7 of the Eastern Conference Finals in Miami.

MISSION ACCOMPLISHED

The Pistons didn't even care that the last team to win the NBA title on the road was 27 years ago, when the Washington Bullets defeated the Seattle SuperSonics — or that the visitor has won in only three instances in the 15 times Game 7 has been played.

"We hear all that stuff, but we don't pay attention to it," Piston guard Lindsey Hunter said. "We feel like all those stats and stuff doesn't mean anything. It all comes down to what you do between those lines. And, that's how we play. People start throwing numbers at us: 'This team hasn't done this or no team has done that.' We don't care about that."

The apprehension and anxiousness in San Antonio was understandable. Not only did the Spurs become the first team to fail to win a Game 6 clincher at home, but the Spurs top three players, Tim Duncan, Tony Parker and Ginobili, weren't exactly lighting it up down the stretch. In the fourth quarter of Games 5 and 6, Parker had a total of three points, Ginobili hit three of 12 shots from the field, and Duncan converted only four of 13 free throws.

No one absorbed more of the criticism for the Spurs' uneven play in the last four games of the series than Duncan, whose two Finals MVP performances appeared to be virtually erased from the critics' memories. Many questioned Duncan's ability to lead his team. It took Spurs head coach Gregg Popovich to provide the proper perspective the day before the biggest game in franchise history.

"We forgot about Tim," Popovich said, "he didn't forget about anything."

The Spurs made sure not to repeat the Game 6 mistakes, when Duncan rarely touched the ball in the fourth quarter. In the first half of the biggest game of his or any of his teammates' and coaches' careers, Duncan had 13 field goal attempts. Even though he missed 10 of them, it was just a matter of time before he broke through, which is exactly

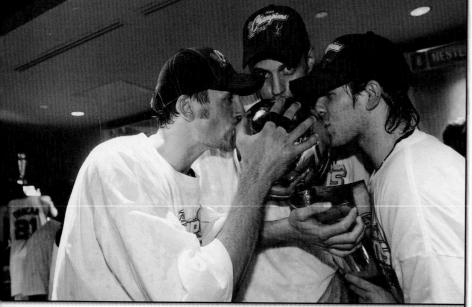

what happened in the third quarter. Trailing by nine points and having missed their first six shots to begin the third, the Spurs were on the verge of being buried when Duncan emerged, ending a 13-minute, 58-second scoring drought as he poured in 12 points and grabbed six rebounds.

The fourth quarter belonged to the Spurs as Ginobili brought the capacity crowd to its feet with a twisting dunk to break the tie with 10 minutes left in the game. Robert Horry and Bruce Bowen then followed up with consecutive three-pointers.

When the gap closed to four, 69-65, it was Duncan, surrounded by a wall of Pistons, who found Ginobili open for a 26-foot momentum-killing three-pointer, giving the Spurs a seven-point lead and a reason to celebrate with a little less than three minutes remaining. The Pistons never got within four, thanks to the Spurs' defense, which held the Pistons to 35 points in the second half, 17 in the fourth, highlighted by Bowen's block of Chauncey Billups' three-point attempt with 55 seconds remaining. The Spurs held to a 73-68 lead before winning 81-74.

"I don't know how the hell we did it, but I don't care," said Popovich during the trophy presentation on center court.

The Spurs' Game 7 triumph and the 2005 NBA Championship was a result of a total team effort. Ginobili was sensational, scoring 23 points — 11 in the fourth quarter — and Horry came up huge with 15 points in 32 minutes.

But, it was Duncan's assertiveness and his ability to will himself and his teammates to the championship. He demanded the ball in the most crucial situations, and that made the ultimate difference — Duncan scored 17 of his 25 points in the second half.

"You follow your leader," Spurs guard Tony Parker said. "Timmy is the leader of the team, and he just carried us tonight."

By George Gervin

The Finger Roll
Silencing the Critics, Championship Style

Game 7 featured a low-scoring first half with both teams jockeying for position. But, then, in the third quarter, "Mr. MVP" Tim Duncan, took over. Once he started getting assertive, everybody else was motivated. He took a lot of shots and that is unusual for him. But, he showed the guys that he was there to play.

The Pistons struggled when Chauncey Billups and Rasheed Wallace got into foul trouble in the first half. When you are one of the main guys, you sometimes have to let guys go and let them get two points. With all the foul trouble, Detroit just could not be as aggressive.

The Spurs played well as a unit, especially in the third quarter when they really started cooking. Nazr Mohammed made some good blocks. Bruce Bowen played strong defense, and Manu Ginobili was able to penetrate and get a couple dunks.

All that started with the MVP, Tim Duncan. He just knows how to win. A lot of people were talking about how soft he is and how he needs to do this and he needs to do that — all he needs to do is be Tim Duncan. He has answered all of the critics who were making all that noise and questioning his ability and his assertiveness.

This was a great series for basketball. This was a classic matchup, and we should be proud of both teams. The Pistons did not really lose because they worked hard; they came back from some serious deficits, and they never gave up. You also have to give Larry Brown a lot of credit. The Pistons really wanted to go out and win it for him.

But, Spurs head coach Gregg Popovich did an amazing job. He does not like to blow his own horn, but he prepares his team and gives his guys direction. He has put San Antonio on the map for winning championships. We have always had a winning tradition, but now we are proud to have a true dynasty.

STARTERS	POS	MIN	FGM-A	3PM-A	FTM-A	OF-R	DF-R	T-R	AST	STL	BLK	TO	PF	PTS
Bruce Bowen	SF	41	2-4	1-1	0-0	0	4	4	1	0	1	1	5	5
Tim Duncan	FC	42	10-27	0-0	5-6	5	6	11	3	0	2	5	2	25
Nazr Mohammed	C	22	0-3	0-0	0-0	1	6	7	0	0	2	0	3	0
Tony Parker	PG	38	3-11	1-3	1-2	0	2	2	3	0	0	1	4	8
Manu Ginobili	SG	35	8-13	2-2	5-5	0	5	5	4	1	0	3	3	23
Bench														
Brent Barry	G	29	2-3	1-1	0-0	0	4	4	2	2	1	2	2	5
Robert Horry	PF	32	4-7	2-4	5-6	2	3	5	1	1	1	1	1	15
Tony Massenburg	FC	DNP	Coach's Decision											
Glenn Robinson	SF	DNP	Coach's Decision											
Rasho Nesterovic	C	DNP	Coach's Decision											
Beno Udrih	PG	DNP	Coach's Decision											
TOTALS			29-68	7-11	16-19	8	30	38	14	4	7	13	20	81
			42.6%	63.6%	84.2%				Team TO (pts off): 13 (15)					
			46.8%	47.1%	68.4%				Team TO (pts off): 5 (6)					

STARTERS	POS	MIN	FGM-A	3PM-A	FTM-A	OF-R	DF-R	T-R	AST	STL	BLK	TO	PF	PTS
Tayshaun Prince	SF	41	4-13	1-4	0-0	1	1	2	1	2	0	1	1	9
Rasheed Wallace	FC	28	5-10	1-4	0-0	0	1	1	1	2	1	1	5	11
Ben Wallace	FC	38	6-10	0-0	0-2	2	9	11	1	2	2	0	5	12
Chauncey Billups	PG	40	3-8	0-3	7-8	1	3	4	8	1	0	1	4	13
Richard Hamilton	SG	46	6-18	0-2	3-4	1	7	8	1	0	1	1	3	15
BENCH														
Lindsey Hunter	PG	21	2-8	0-1	0-0	0	1	1	2	1	0	0	2	4
Antonio McDyess	PF	23	5-7	0-0	0-0	3	4	7	2	0	2	2	4	10
Elden Campbell	C	1	0-0	0-0	0-0	0	0	0	1	0	0	0	0	0
Ronald Dupree	SF	1	0-0	0-0	0-0	0	0	0	0	0	0	0	0	0
Darvin Ham	SF	1	0-0	0-0	0-0	0	0	0	0	0	0	0	0	0
Carlos Arroyo	PG	DNP	Coach's Decision											
Darko Milicic	FC	DNP	Coach's Decision											
TOTALS			31-74	2-14	10-14	8	26	34	17	8	6	6	24	74
			41.9%	14.3%	71.4%				Team TO (pts off): 9 (4)